B.

Network Project with HP Switch

A step by step guide to your network project

First Edition

Copyright © 2016 by B. T. Ricci

All rights reserved. No part of this publication may be reproduced, distributed, or transmitted in any form or by any means, including photocopying, recording, or other electronic or mechanical methods, without the prior written permission of the publisher.

ISBN: 978-1-535-29387-7

To J.J. with all my love.

- B. T. Ricci

Subscribe to our youtube channel for free access to video tutorials.

Subscribe to our fan page for free access to extra chapters.

Youtube - Facebook

Summary

INTRODUCTION 1
    Book Content 1
    Target Audience 2
    About the Author 2
    Youtube Channel & Website 2
    Conclusion 3

NETWORK PROJECT 4
    Stakeholders 4
    Project Requirements 6
    Project Scope 7
    Switch Model 8
    Project Closure 9
    Conclusion 9

INITIAL SETUP 11
    Physical Connection 11
    Accessing the Console 12
    Setting an IP Address 15
    Secret Command-Line Interface 17
    Access Recovery 19
    Conclusion 20

POST-INSTALLATION 21
    Changing the Default Password 21
    Firmware Upgrade 22
    Changing the Hostname 24
    Setting Date and Time 25
    Centralizing the Log Files 26

- Conclusion 27
- **ACCESS MANAGEMENT** 28
  - Creating a User Group 28
  - Creating a User 30
  - Enabling Remote Access 33
  - Conclusion 37
- **VIRTUAL NETWORK** 39
  - Creating a Vlan 39
  - Vlan Configuration 41
  - Trunk Configuration 43
  - Hybrid Configuration 46
  - Conclusion 49
- **ROUTING BETWEEN VLANS** 50
  - Initial Setup 50
  - Setting an IP Address 53
  - Device Types 55
  - Step by Step Guide 56
  - Vlan Creation 56
  - Virtual Interface Creation 57
  - Setting the Default Route 60
  - DHCP Server Installation 60
  - Conclusion 64
- **VOICE OVER IP** 65
  - Creating a Voice Vlan 65
  - Voice Vlan Configuration 66
  - Conclusion 73
- **PERFORMANCE & REDUNDANCY** 74
  - Link Aggregation – Trunk Mode 74
  - Link Aggregation – Access Mode 78
  - Link Aggregation – Windows 2012 83
  - Conclusion 84

CENTRALIZED AUTHENTICATION ... 86
Step by Step Guide ... 86
Creating a User Group ... 87
Radius Server Installation ... 90
Radius Server Configuration ... 91
Setting Radius Authentication ... 101
Conclusion ... 104

NETWORK MONITORING ... 106
SNMP Configuration ... 106
SNMPv3 Configuration ... 109
Conclusion ... 113

PORT MONITORING ... 115
Port Mirroring ... 115
Conclusion ... 118

PACKET FILTER ... 120
Step by Step Guide ... 120
Access List Creation ... 121
Access Class Creation ... 123
Behavior Creation ... 125
Create Access Policy ... 126
Applying the Access Policy ... 128
Conclusion ... 129

BANDWIDTH LIMITATION ... 130
Traffic Shaping ... 130
Conclusion ... 132

DEVICE ISOLATION ... 133
Configuring Port Isolation ... 133
Conclusion ... 135

VIRTUAL LABORATORY ... 136
Step by Step Guide ... 136
VirtualBox Installation ... 137

Wireshark Installation..137
HP Network Simulator Installation 139
Using the Network Simulator 140
Conclusion 142
Afterword..144

INTRODUCTION

Despite having a good knowledge related to computer networks and even have some certifications on the subject, Luke, a 26-year-old IT analyst has just received a mission to deploy a new network using only HP switches.

Despite being confident in his skills, Luke realizes that he does not know how to configure this brand of equipment and after researching this subject for a while was able to notice a lack of such documentation on the market.

The lack of such documentation was the inspiration to write this book which aims to teach in a practical way how to perform the installation and configuration of a network using HP switches.

Throughout this book, we will follow all stages of Luke's story, which in addition to the installation of a new corporate network will also be responsible for its operation at the end of the project.

This book can be used in a couple of ways. If you read it in a linear way, you will follow the story of Luke, learn how to configure network equipment, how to troubleshoot network issues, how to improve your network environment already established and how to create a virtual laboratory.

If you don't want to read in a linear way, each chapter also works individually. Therefore, you can just skip to a particular section and use the book as a reference material.

Book Content

To improve the learning curve, the reader will be introduced to real life examples involving challenges related to the deployment and operation of a computer network.

This book focuses on teaching through practical examples, therefore to each problem presented it will show two different ways to perform the same configuration and achieve the expected result.

First, the book will demonstrate how to perform the configuration of a switch using it's web interface. Second, the book will explain how to do the same configuration using the command-line.

At the end of this book the reader will be able to:

- Create a list of network project requirements
- Choose the correct switch model based on the project requirements list
- Update the firmware version of a switch

- Perform the initial setup of a switch through the console
- Enable remote access to a switch through telnet, ssh or http
- Integrate the remote access authentication to the active directory domain
- Set different access levels to a switch
- Perform network segmentation through the use of vlans
- Connect switches through the use of a trunk
- Enable routing between vlans
- Add redundancy and improve performance through the aggregation of links
- Filter unwanted traffic and limit the bandwidth utilization
- Monitor the network traffic via SNMP and port mirroring
- Create a virtual laboratory to perform configuration tests
- Concentrate all log files on a Syslog server
- Setup a DHCP server
- Recover access to the switch if the password is forgotten

Target Audience

This book is written for a specific audience. Professionals in the information technology field who have some knowledge of computer networks and want to deploy or operate a medium-sized network using HP switches.

About the Author

B. T. Ricci works with information technology in the areas of network and information security for over 15 years. He has numerous network projects deployed over 13 countries and currently works as an information technology manager at the defense department.

Among his qualifications, he has certifications related to computer networks like CCNP and CCDP, certifications related to information security like CISSP, CBCP, and CCSP, certifications related to project management like PMP and PMI-RMP, his MCSE certification related to Microsoft Windows and LPIC2 related to Linux.

Youtube Channel & Website

Over the years, after becoming a manager I was able to notice that my time was being consumed more and more by administrative tasks and less on technical tasks.

The gradual removal of technical tasks from my schedule bothered me because this was always my favorite part of the job, so I started looking for a way to keep me technically relevant using my free time.

INTRODUCTION

The desire to keep my technical knowledge relevant made me create a youtube channel called **FuckingIT** where I present purely technical videos related to networks and servers.

After the first year, it was possible to notice that users of the channel were requesting to be able to copy the commands shown in the videos from somewhere and this was the reason to create the fucking-it.com website.

The reader should watch our channel's videos related to the configuration of HP switches to speed up his learning.

The reader should visit our website to check for updates, extra material, or messages related to the book.

Conclusion

In the end, I hope you have an enjoyable experience that adds value to your work and helps you achieve your goals. If you have any questions or have found an error in this material, go to our website and send me a message.

– Chapter 01 –

NETWORK PROJECT

After a long selection process, Luke was the candidate selected for the network analyst position by Mark, the manager of the information technology department. As his first assignment, a modest budget was made available that should be able to cover the cost of deploying a new network using managed switches.

By having some knowledge related to project management, Luke knows that in order to succeed in the implementation of this project he will need to combine his technical skills with some project management skills.

Throughout this chapter, the following tasks related to project management will be presented: stakeholder management, project requirements, project scope and project closure.

All the lessons included in this chapter will be presented in a practical way using Luke's point of view during the implementation of his project.

Stakeholders

Usually, stakeholders are individuals or companies that have an interest in your project. Normally, these entities can affect, or be affected positively or negatively by your project.

A stakeholder registry is a tool that can help in the success of your project. By documenting who are the most influential people, and how to communicate effectively with these individuals, it is possible to reduce the risk of failure and increase the likelihood of success for your project.

In our example, Luke, knowing this tool, generated a spreadsheet with the following fields.

- ID
- Name
- Description
- Level of Influence
- Type
- Expectations
- Contact Information

As an example, here is a sample of the stakeholder registry created by Luke for his network project.

ID – 001
Name – Mark P
Description – IT Manager
Level of influence – High
Type – Positive
Expectations – Increase the speed of the network from 100Mbps to 1Gbps
Contact Information – mark.ti@fucking-it.com

ID – 002
Name – Roy P
Description – Linux Specialist
Level of influence – Average
Type – Positive
Expectations – Integrate the new switches with the existing monitoring tool
Contact Information – 55 11 2555-6677

ID – 003
Name – Leia S
Description – IT Support Analyst
Level of influence – Average
Type – Negative
Expectations – She wants to prove that the new network is not required and will try to find flaws in the project
Contact Information – leia.ti@fucking-it.com

Keep in mind that a positive stakeholder can see the benefit that the project will bring to the company, or to his work and usually is interested in helping the project implementation.

On the other hand, a negative stakeholder cannot see, feel threatened, or simply do not want the benefit provided by the project, and may offer resistance.

Try to imagine the chances of success if the IT manager and Luke argue about the project priorities aggressively during a public meeting. At this time, it is possible that Mark becomes a negative stakeholder and stop offering his support, which is essential to the success of the project.

As a result, you should always try to influence positive stakeholders to remain at your side while you try to influence the negative stakeholders in a way they become neutral, or perhaps even positive stakeholders.

Project Requirements

In order to understand what must be delivered at the end of the project, you must map the project requirements, either through meetings with stakeholders or in any other way possible.

A project requirement is a statement that identifies a feature, capacity or quality that the new network *must have.*

As an example, we might mention that the technology manager during a meeting with Luke reported a need for the new network to have at least two vlans in order to separate the servers network from the workstations network.

It should be clear that not every requirement will be 100% technical, as an example, we could mention that Rick, the president of the company, will receive a major client on December 18 and because of that he determined that the project should be completed by December 14.

If the requirements are not properly registered, the delivered project may not add the expected value for the customer and therefore be considered a failure. Imagine that the project was completed only on December 19 and for this reason the company did not have access to the internet on the day that the President received the visit of his most important client.

The *requirement registration* is a tool that can help in the success of your project. If you document the requirements and associate each one with a stakeholder, you will be able to prioritize the tasks by its level of importance.

In our example, Luke, knowing this tool, generated a spreadsheet with the following fields.

- ID
- Requirement
- Stakeholder
- Status

As an example, here is a sample of the requirement registry created by Luke for his network project.

ID – 001
Requirement – All switch interfaces must provide the speed of 1Gbps.
Stakeholder – Mark, IT Manager
Status – Approved

ID – 002
Requirement – The switches must offer dynamic routing functionality

Stakeholder – Roy, Linux Specialist
Status – Denied

ID – 003
Requirement – The switches must support the use of vlans
Stakeholder – Bill, Windows Specialist
Status – Approved

ID – 004
Requirement – Servers and workstations must be located in different vlans
Stakeholder – Bill, Windows Specialist
Status – Approved

As a result, the project now has a direction to be followed and goals to be met that will actually add value to the customer while helping you to keep track of all work that needs to be done.

Notice that each requirement should be associated with a requester stakeholder and thus provide a direction about to whom should be requested the validation of each one of the approved requirements, or to whom should we report about requirements that have not been approved after due evaluation.

In our example, Luke would notify the requester Roy that his requirement was not approved due to the dynamic routing feature not be considered essential for the project of the new computer network.

As a result, you should try to register and prioritize all the requirements of the network project without forgetting to keep every stakeholder informed about the approval or disapproval of their requirements.

Project Scope

Once all the stakeholders and their requirements have been listed you will be able to analyze the approved requirements and reach an agreement about the project scope definition.

The scope must document what will be part of the project. Therefore, you must analyze previously registered requirements and reach an agreement about what are the deliverables of the project.

In our example, Luke and the project stakeholders were able to agree on the following definition of scope: "Creating a new computer network that meets the technical specifications recorded in the document called ***requirements of the new network***".

Network Project with HP Switch

Here is the list of approved requirements included in the document called requirements of the new network.

- The project must use 03 managed switches
- Each network switch must have at least 48 network interfaces
- All network switch interfaces must offer the speed of 1Gbps
- It must be possible to manage each switch through a console cable
- It must be possible to manage each switch remotely via telnet, ssh, and http
- It must be possible to integrate the authentication with active directory
- It must be possible to configure different levels of access to the switches
- The company's servers should be isolated in an exclusive vlan
- The company's workstations should be isolated in an exclusive vlan
- The company's phones should be isolated in an exclusive vlan
- External visitors should have their laptops isolated in an exclusive vlan
- A switch should be elected as the main network switch
- The main network switch must provide routing between vlans
- The main network switch must be configured as dhcp server
- The company's workstations must receive the IP address from a dhcp server
- The company's phones must receive the IP address from a dhcp server
- External visitors must receive the IP address from a dhcp server
- The connection between the network switches must be redundant
- The connection between the switch and the file server must be redundant
- All network switches must have their firmware updated
- All network switches must redirect their logs to a Syslog server
- It must be possible to limit the bandwidth used by a switch interface
- It must be possible to block access to specific IP addresses through rules
- It must be possible to monitor the network switches via SNMP
- It must be possible to monitor the network traffic through mirroring
- A VoIP phone must have its voice vlan automatically configured
- A VoIP phone must be able to connect a workstation to the network
- A virtual laboratory must be installed in order to test settings outside of the production environment

In order to verify that the project was successfully implemented, Luke should compare the results of his project with the agreed list of specifications that were recorded in the document called ***requirements of the new network***.

Switch Model

After finishing the scope definition, Luke could compare the technical requirements of the project with the technical specifications of multiple switch models available on the manufacturer's website.

Because it is a medium-sized network and has only a modest budget available, Luke came to the conclusion that he could use the switch models 1910 and A5500 to meet the project scope requirements.

The switch model 1910 will be used in the access layer to connect end devices such as workstations, phones, printers and visitors computers.

Because it offers advanced routing features, the switch model A5500 will be used in the core layer to connect servers, provide routing between vlans and act as a dhcp server.

Project Closure

Nowadays, it is very common to find IT professionals who treat the project as finished, incorrectly, after completing only the technical part of the job defined in project scope.

A project can only be considered complete when it is formally accepted by the customer, this means that at the end of the project you should get a formal approval confirming that all approved requirements of the new network were delivered successfully according to the project scope.

Keep in mind that the person responsible for the technical implementation of the project may not be the same person who will manage the new network environment on a daily basis. For this reason, you should consider adding a knowledge transfer phase that can be done through training, through the delivery of a project documentation, or a combination of both options.

At the end of the project, we could say that all the knowledge related to the implementation of the new network is centralized inside Luke's mind, and it is his responsibility to document the new network environment, transfer his knowledge to other members of the company and avoid the risk of information loss in case something happens to him.

As a result, finish your project in the right way and prove to be a great professional by presenting incontestable records that all approved requirements were delivered successfully together with a knowledge transfer phase required for the administration of the new network environment.

Conclusion

This chapter taught using practical examples how to do some major project management tasks to help a successful implementation of a network project.

The reader should understand that a good technical knowledge used together with basic project management techniques can significantly increase the chances of success.

At the end of this chapter, the reader should be able to map the relevant stakeholders and their project requirements, in order define the project scope and begin the technical implementation.

– Chapter 02 –

INITIAL SETUP

After purchasing the network switches needed for his project and wait a short delivery period, Luke received and installed his new network switches within a rack of his data center.

A network environment with manageable switches offers several advantages, however before a network administrator get these advantages, he needs to perform an initial setup phase.

This chapter will teach how to perform the initial configuration on a switch through a detailed step by step approach.

Throughout this chapter, the following tasks related to the implementation of the network project will be presented:

- How to setup a computer to access a manageable switch
- How to do the first access to a switch through the console
- How to do the first access to a switch through the web interface
- How to setup an IP address on a switch
- How to access the secret command line of the 1910 model
- How to recover access to a switch

All the lessons included in this chapter will be presented in a practical way using Luke's point of view during the implementation of his project.

The reader should be aware that there are several models of HP network switches. Therefore, it is possible that the initial setup shown using the switch model 1910 as its base, are not applicable to the model used by the reader.

The *sixth chapter* of this book is responsible for providing an alternative way to perform the initial setup on other switch models like the A5500, that will be used as the main switch of this project.

Physical Connection

After finishing the physical installation of the device into the rack, you must connect a computer on the network switch management interface through a cable known as *console cable.*

The console cable has two different types of connectors and is supplied together with a new switch, therefore, you should connect the serial interface to a computer and the RJ45 interface on the switch port labeled as *console*.

If the computer being used does not have a serial interface available, you can use an usb to serial interface adapter as long as the adapter driver is installed correctly.

The connection between a computer and the console interface is usually used to perform a basic initial setup, like setting an administrative address for remote access, or setting the default equipment password.

Accessing the Console

After finishing the physical connection between a computer and the switch console interface, you will need to use a specific software to access the command-line interface of the switch through a serial connection.

Putty is a free software that can be used to connect physically or remotely on the command-line of a network switch in order to proceed with the device setup, therefore, visit the *putty.org* website and download *putty*.

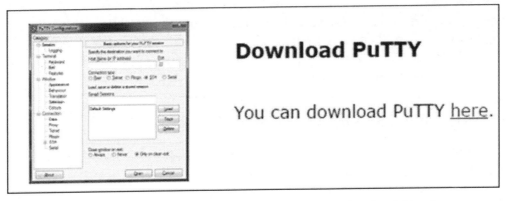

After finishing the download, run the software and wait for the following screen.

INITIAL SETUP

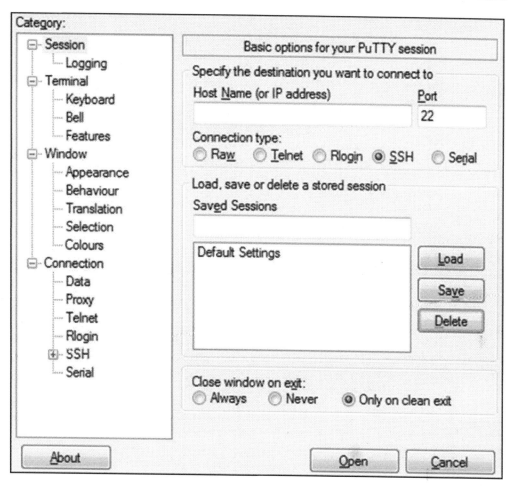

For the computer to be able to communicate with this switch model through a console cable you will need to customize the connection settings, therefore after opening *putty*, select the category named **serial** and change the following parameters.

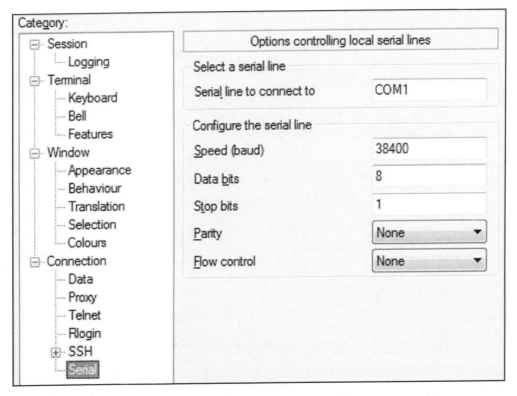

The **Serial line** option specifies which communication port that the computer should use to communicate with the network switch. In our example, it was decided that the computer should use the communication port COM1 to contact the switch.

Notice that the number of the communication port being used may vary, therefore, if the *com1* communication port does not work, try to use the next communication port *com2*, and so on.

The **Speed option** determines the transmission rate that should be used to communicate with the network switch. In our example, the speed was set to use a 38400 bits transfer rate as indicated by the product manual.

Notice that the manual of the network switch should be consulted because different switch models may require different connection speeds. In our example, while the switch model 1910 uses the communication speed of 38400 the A5500 model uses the speed of 9600.

The **Data bits** option specifies the amount of bits containing information that can be sent at once to the network switch. In our example, the option was set to use 8 bits, as indicated by the product manual.

The **Stop bits** option specifies the number of bits that should be used to signal a break or an end in the communication with the network switch. In our example, the option was set to use only a single bit, as indicated by the product manual.

INITIAL SETUP

The ***Parity*** option was formerly used to detect communication failures due to interference, but currently, this parameter is no longer used. In our example, it was determined that the parity should not be used.

The ***Flow control*** parameter was formerly used to set which flow control mechanism should be utilized but currently, this parameter is no longer used. In our example, it was determined that the flow control should not be used.

After setting all the parameters of the serial connection as shown, go to the session category, select the ***Serial*** connection type option and click on the ***Open*** button to start the communication between the network switch and the computer.

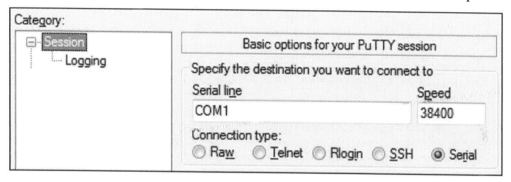

After clicking on the ***Open*** button, the software must connect to the switch and present the initial login screen, where you must enter the ***admin*** username and leave the password field blank.

```
**************************************************************
* Copyright (c) 2010-2015 Hewlett-Packard Development Company, L.P.
* Without the owner's prior written consent,
* no decompiling or reverse-engineering shall be allowed.
**************************************************************
Login authentication
Username:admin
Password:
```

In our example, the network administrator performed the initial access to the command-line of a switch through its console interface using the Putty software and a console cable.

Setting an IP Address

During the initial setup phase, the network administrator will have to define an administrative IP address that will be used to access the equipment remotely.

After successfully log in to the network switch, you will be presented with a basic command-line interface that provides some of the administrative commands available.

Network Project with HP Switch

In order to configure an administrative IP address on the network switch, enter the command *ipsetup* followed by the desired IP address, its network mask and default gateway address.

`# ipsetup ip-address 192.168.1.11 255.255.255.0 default-gateway 192.168.1.1`

After finishing the address configuration, verify the configured IP address on your network switch through the *summary* command which is responsible for presenting a basic summary of the device configuration.

`# summary`

In our example, a network switch model 1910 was configured to use the 192.168.1.11 address, the network mask 255.255.255.0 and the default gateway 192.168.1.1.

To test the setup, you should set an IP address of the same network on a computer and connect it to any port of the network switch.

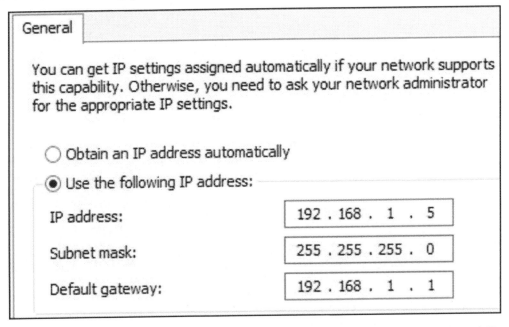

After connecting your computer to a switch port, access the command-line interface of your switch and attempt a connectivity test between the computer and the switch using the *ping* command.

`# ping 192.168.1.5`

After finishing the configuration and the connectivity test between the devices, open your browser, type the IP address of the network switch and access its web interface.

INITIAL SETUP

On the web interface initial login screen, enter the **admin** username, leave the password field in blank and enter the verification code displayed on the screen.

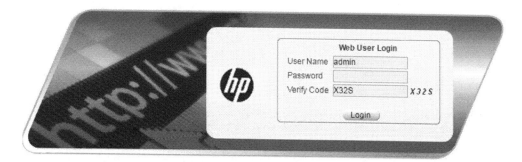

After a successful login, save the network switch settings by clicking on the **Save** option available at the top right of the screen.

In our example, we showed how to perform the configuration of an administrative IP address using the command-line interface; we also showed how to access the web interface and how to save the network switch configuration.

Secret Command-Line Interface

By default, the command-line offered by some of the network switch models provide access to a very limited group of commands that can be seen by pressing the *question mark key*, as shown below.

```
# ?
User view commands:
  initialize   Delete the startup configuration file and reboot system
  ipsetup      Assign an IP address to VLAN-interface 1
  password     Specify password of local user
  ping         Ping function
  quit         Exit from current command view
  reboot       Reboot system/board/card
  summary      Display summary information of the device.
  telnet       Establish one TELNET connection
  upgrade      Upgrade the system boot file, the Boot ROM program or the PoE
               program
```

Some network switch models such as the 1910, offers a hidden feature that allows the network administrator to access a complete list of administrative commands through the command-line.

Network Project with HP Switch

In order to have access to all available commands, use the *cmdline-mode* command and enter the default password specific to your HP switch model.

```
# cmdline-mode on
```

In our example, the password *512900* was used because this is the secret command-line password for the HP switch model 1910.

Keep in mind that **only a subset of HP switch models** have the secret command-line feature available, and each one requires the use of a different secret command-line password.

After entering the secret mode correctly, press the *question mark key* and check the number of commands available.

```
# ?
```

```
User view commands:
  archive         Specify archive settings
  backup          Backup next startup-configuration file to TFTP server
  boot-loader     Set boot loader
  bootrom         Update/read/backup/restore bootrom
  cd              Change current directory
  clock           Specify the system clock
  cluster         Run cluster command
  copy            Copy from one file to another
  crypto-digest   Compute the hash digest for a specified file
  debugging       Enable system debugging functions
  delete          Delete a file
  dir             List files on a file system
  display         Display current system information
  fixdisk         Recover lost chains in storage device
  format          Format the device
  free            Clear user terminal interface
  ftp             Open FTP connection
  initialize      Delete the startup configuration file and reboot system
  ipc             Interprocess communication
  ipsetup         Assign an IP address to VLAN-interface 1
  lock            Lock current user terminal interface
```

After entering this mode, you can save the switch settings by using the *save* command and pressing the **Y** key to confirm your decision.

```
# save
```

In order to verify the complete configuration of a network switch, use the *display current-configuration* command, as shown below.

```
# display current-configuration
```

In our example, we showed how to access the secret command-line feature on an HP network switch model 1910.

INITIAL SETUP

Access Recovery

Although new Switches were purchased to Luke's project, the purchase of used equipment is a very common practice in the market.

In case a used equipment is purchased, the network administrator needs to know how to perform the access recovery procedure, in order to have administrative access to the device.

The access recovery procedure should be carried out if the switch password has been lost or forgotten for some reason.

First, turn off the switch, plug a console cable between the switch and a computer, open the Putty software and access the device console, as shown before.

While the network switch is booting, press the key sequence **[Ctrl + B]** to access the boot menu.

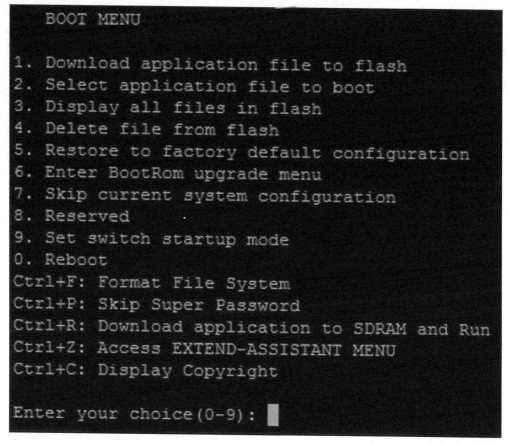

On the boot menu screen, select the option **7** to tell the system to ignore the current configuration saved in the switch and press the **Y** key to confirm your decision.

19

On the boot menu screen, enter the option **0** to reboot the switch immediately.

After the switch is restarted, it will ignore its saved configuration file; the network administrator should then use the *initialize* command to reset the switch to its factory default configuration.

```
# initialize
```

After pressing **Y**, the switch will delete the saved configuration file and reset to factory default settings which use the *admin* username and an *empty password*.

In our example, we showed how to recover access to a network switch, after losing or forgetting its password.

Conclusion

This chapter taught through some practical examples how to perform the initial setup of a network switch, in order to help the network administrator access the switch configuration interface.

Throughout this chapter, we were able to follow Luke while he did the initial setup of the switches purchased for the implementation of the network project.

At the end of this chapter, the reader should be able to perform the initial setup of a network switch.

To improve the learning curve, the following videos were published on our youtube channel showing how to use the techniques presented in this chapter:

- HP Switch – Initial IP Configuration
- HP Switch – Password Recovery

– Chapter 03 –

POST-INSTALLATION

After finishing the initial setup, Luke is able to proceed with the implementation of his network project and configure the switches using the command-line or the web interface.

However, before diving into the switch configuration, the network administrator should consider performing a post-installation phase, in order to enhance the device information security level.

This chapter will teach how to perform the post-installation phase on a switch through a detailed step by step approach.

Throughout this chapter, the following tasks related to the implementation of the network project will be presented:

- How to change the default password
- How to upgrade the firmware
- How to set the correct date and time
- How to change the hostname
- How to redirect the logs to a Syslog server

All the lessons included in this chapter will be presented in a practical way using Luke's point of view during the implementation of his project.

Changing the Default Password

As the post-installation first step, the network administrator should change the default password of his equipment, keep in mind that at this point the switch might still be using the factory default password for the administrative user.

Open the web interface, select the **Authentication** menu and click on the **Users** option to be sent to the local users and groups management page.

In order to change the default password of the administrative user, select the **Local Users** tab, locate the **admin** user and click on the **modify** operation icon.

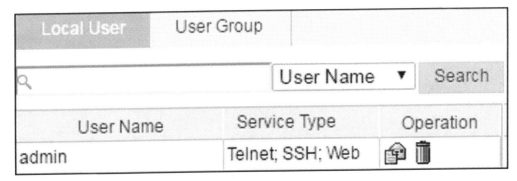

On the user properties screen, select the **Modify password** checkbox, enter a new password and click on the **Apply button**.

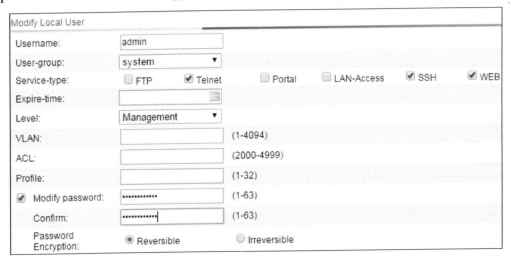

In order to test your configuration, click on the **Logout** option available at the top right of the screen and try to log in again to the web interface using the new password of the admin user.

After changing the password, be sure to save your settings by clicking on the **Save** option available at the top right of the screen.

Firmware Upgrade

As the post-installation second step, the network administrator should update the firmware used by his equipment, keep in mind that at this point the switch might be using the factory default version of firmware which may have security flaws.

In order to download the updated version of firmware, go to the HP Enterprise website at **hpe.com**. If you have any trouble finding the correct firmware, go to **google.com** and search for "**HP Networking support search tool**" which is a tool that will help you find the correct firmware for your switch.

On the search tool, you will have to enter model or the part number of the switch

POST-INSTALLATION

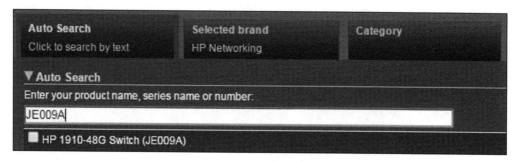

The part number is a standard way to reference equipment established by the manufacturer itself where each device or piece of equipment is assigned a unique identification.

In our example, we downloaded the last firmware version for the switch model 1910-48G by entering the part number JE009A on the searching tool.

After downloading the new firmware, extract it from the compressed file, in order to continue the firmware upgrade process.

As the next step, access the web interface of your switch and log in using an account with administrative privileges.

On the web interface, select the *Device* menu and click on the *Device maintenance* option to be sent to the software upgrade screen where you will need to choose the new firmware file to be used.

23

After finishing the upgrade, the switch will reboot, and the login screen will be displayed.

In our example, the firmware of a 1910-48G switch was updated successfully.

After finishing the upgrade, open the web interface, select the **Summary** menu, click the **System Information** option and make sure to check if the new firmware version is being listed on the right part of the screen.

Changing the Hostname

As the post-installation third step, the network administrator should change the device identification name, keep in mind that at this point the switch might be using the factory default hostname.

Open the web interface, select the **Device** menu and click on the **Basic** option to be sent to the switch basic administration screen.

To change the device name, select the **System Name** tab, look for the **Sysname** option, modify the hostname of the switch and click on the **Apply** button.

After setting the hostname successfully, the new device identification name should appear on the top left of the web interface of your switch.

In our example, the network administrator used the following hostnames to keep the network environment organized: *fkit-sw01*, *fkit-sw02* and *fkit-sw03*.

In the next tab, the network administrator is able to set an idle session timeout to the web interface, therefore, select the **Web Idle Timeout** tab and enter the number of minutes that a session can remain idle before it is automatically closed.

POST-INSTALLATION

In our example, the network administrator set 5 minutes as idle session timeout limit.

Setting Date and Time

As the post-installation fourth step, the network administrator should configure the correct date and time on the switch, either manually or automatically through the use of the NTP protocol.

Keep in mind the importance of setting the correct date and time, because when the network administrator needs to solve a problem, his first reliable source of information should be the switch's log file and this information is stored based on the system clock.

In order to configure the switch date and time manually, select the **Device** menu and click on the **System time** option to be sent to the configuration screen.

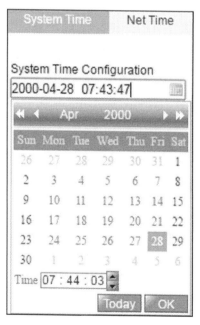

In order to set the automatic date and time configuration, access the **Net Team** tab, choose the switch *interface* that will connect to the NTP server, set a *query*

25

interval in seconds, enter the IP address of the NTP server, select the ***desired time zone*** and click on the *Apply* button.

In our example, the network administrator configured a Switch to get date and time configuration automatically from the NTP server ***200.160.7.186*** every ***64 seconds*** and use a time zone of *-3*.

After finishing the configuration, go back to the *System time* tab and make sure the date and time were updated.

Centralizing the Log Files

As the post-installation last step, the network administrator should configure the switches to centralize the log files on a Syslog server.

If a switch by any reason stops working, the network administrator will have no clue about what happened because he will not have access to the log file, however, if the log files were being sent to a Syslog server the network administrator could easily use the log stored on the server to help solve the issue.

Open the web interface, select the *Device* menu and click on the *Syslog* option to be sent to the log administration screen.

In order to send the device log over the network, access the *Loghost* tab, select the *IPV4* option, enter the IP address of the Syslog server and click on the *Apply* button.

From this moment on, all log records will be sent to the computer using the IP address 192.168.1.15 through the network, therefore, this computer needs to have a Syslog software installed.

Visual Syslog Server for Windows is a free software that can be used to receive Syslog messages on a computer, therefore, visit sourceforge.net and download it.

After finishing the installation, the network administrator will be able to view the log messages sent by the Switch through the graphical interface, as shown below.

In our example, the network administrator configured a switch to send log messages over the network to a computer running a Syslog server software.

Conclusion

This chapter taught using practical examples how to perform a post-installation phase to raise the information security level of a switch.

Throughout this chapter, we were able to follow Luke while he performed the post-installation on a switch and met the following project requirements listed in the document called ***requirements of the new network***.

• All network switches must have their firmware updated
• All network switches must redirect their logs to a Syslog server

At the end of this chapter, the reader should be able to perform the post-installation phase on a network switch.

To improve the learning curve, the following videos were published on our youtube channel showing how to use the techniques presented in this chapter:

• HP Switch – Firmware Upgrade
• HP Switch – Change the Default Password
• HP Switch – Date and Time Configuration
• HP Switch – Hostname Configuration
• HP Switch – Centralizing the Log Files

– Chapter 04 –

ACCESS MANAGEMENT

After finishing the initial setup, Luke decides to enable the remote access to the switches and create the necessary accounts, in order to allow the access of the information technology staff.

The Remote access feature is able to facilitate teamwork, by allowing multiple persons to access a switch, without the need to be physically close to the device.

This chapter will teach how to perform the account management and enable remote access through a detailed step by step approach.

Throughout this chapter, the following tasks related to the implementation of the network project will be presented:

- How to create a user group
- How to create a user account
- How to enable remote access

All the lessons included in this chapter will be presented in a practical way using Luke's point of view during the implementation of his project.

Creating a User Group

After a brief planning, it was decided that two groups of users should exist and offer different access levels to its members who are essentially IT analysts from the information technology staff.

In our example, members of the *fkit-admin* group should have all the administrative permissions available on the network switches while members of the *fkit-users* group should be able to access the device with read-only permissions.

Open the web interface, select the **Authentication** menu and click on the **Users** option to be sent to the local users and groups management page.

In order to create a new user group, select the **User Group** tab and click on the **Add** button.

On the group creation screen, set the desired access level and click on the **Apply** button.

ACCESS MANAGEMENT

Local User	User Group

Add User Group

Group-name:	FKIT-ADMIN
Level:	Management ▼
VLAN:	
ACL:	
User-profile	

During setup of a new group account, the network administrator will need to specify the access level offered to the members of this group, therefore, here we present a list of access levels available and their descriptions.

The *visitor* access level allows its members to access a simpler version of the web interface with read-only permissions, members of this group will be able to perform some basic connectivity tests such as ping and traceroute.

The *monitor* access level allows its members to access a complete version of the web interface with read-only permissions, members of this group will be able to perform some basic connectivity tests such as ping and traceroute.

The *configure* access level allows its members to access a complete version of the web interface with write permissions, however, members of this group will not be able to create new users, upgrade the firmware or to backup and restore the switch configuration file.

The *management* access level allows its members to access a complete version of the web interface with write permissions, without any restrictions.

In our example, the network administrator created two groups. The first group, called *fkit-admins*, received the *management* access level and the second group, called *fkit-users*, received the *monitor* access level.

It is important to highlight that, some switch models do not offer the group configuration on its web interface, however, the network administrator is able to use the command-line, in order to manage the group configuration

After finishing the group setup, be sure to save your settings by clicking on the *Save* option available at the top right of the screen.

If you need to remove an existing group of users, select the **User Group** tab and click on the *trash can* icon next to the group name.

It is possible that some readers prefer to use the command-line instead of the web interface, therefore, we will also teach you how to create a group of users using the command-line.

Using either the console, telnet or ssh, connect to the command-line of your switch and log in with a user who has administrative privileges.

If available to your switch model, enter the *_cmdline-mode* command in order to access the secret command-line mode of the device.

```
# cmdline-mode on
```

Use the *system-view* command to enter the configuration mode.

```
# system-view
```

Create a user group using the following commands.

```
# user-group FKIT-ADMIN
# authorization-attribute level 3

# user-group FKIT-USERS
# authorization-attribute level 1
# quit
```

In order to set the access level of a group you must specify the ***authorization-attribute*** using a numeric format, therefore, you should know that the access levels called visitor, monitor, configure and management use the identification numbers from 0 to 3.

Use the following command to check your configuration.

```
# display user-group
```

Save your settings by using the command below.

```
# save
```

To delete an existing group, enter the configuration mode and use the following command.

```
# undo user-group FKIT-USERS
```

Creating a User

After finishing the group creation, we will show you how to create a new user on a network switch, therefore, open the web interface, select the *Authentication* menu and click on the *Users* option to be sent to the local users and groups management page.

ACCESS MANAGEMENT

In order to create a new user, select the ***Local User*** tab and click on the ***Add*** button.

On the user creation screen, set a ***username***, a ***password***, select the ***group*** created earlier, the type of services that the user should have access and click on the ***Apply*** button.

During the setup of a new account, you will need to set the types of services that the user should be authorized to access, therefore, here we present a list of services available and their descriptions.

The ***FTP*** service-type allows a user to connect remotely to the switch using an FTP client software.

The ***Telnet*** service-type allows a user to connect remotely to the switch using a telnet client software, like Putty.

The ***SSH*** service-type allows a user to connect remotely to the switch using an SSH client software, like Putty.

The ***Web*** service-type allows a user to connect remotely to the switch using a browser software, like Chrome.

The **Portal** service-type allows a user who successfully authenticate himself on a custom web page of the switch to connect to the network.

The **Lan-access** service-type allows a user who successfully authenticate himself on the switch using the 802.1x protocol to connect to the network.

In our example, two accounts were created. The username Luke received the **management** access level because he is a member of the **fkit-admins** group, while the other user received the **monitor** access level for being part of the **fkit-users** group.

In order to test your configuration, click on the **Logout** option available at the top right of the screen, try to log in again to the web interface using one of the accounts previously created and make sure the menus are being displayed in according to the access level configured.

It is important to highlight that, some switch models do not offer the User configuration option under the authentication menu and instead, offer the User configuration option under the Device menu.

After finishing the user setup, be sure to save your settings by clicking on the **Save** option available at the top right of the screen.

If you need to remove an existing user account, select the **Local User** tab and click on the trash can icon next to the username.

It is possible that some readers prefer to use the command-line instead of the web interface, therefore, we will also teach you how to create a user account using the command-line.

Using either the console, telnet or ssh, connect to the command-line of your switch and log in with a user who has administrative privileges.

If available to your switch model, enter the _**cmdline-mode** command in order to access the secret command-line mode of the device.

```
# _cmdline-mode on
```

Use the **system-view** command to enter the configuration mode.

```
# system-view
```

Create a user account using the following commands.

```
# local-user luke
# password simple kamisama123@
# group FKIT-ADMIN
# service-type ssh telnet
# service-type web
```

ACCESS MANAGEMENT

```
# service-type terminal
# quit

# local-user bill
# password simple d0kutodod1a
# group FKIT-USERS
# service-type ssh telnet
# service-type web
# quit
```

In our example, the username luke received the *management* access level and permission to connect to the switch using the *console, ssh, telnet and the web interface*.

In our example, the username bill received the *monitor* access level and permission to connect to the switch using only *ssh, telnet, and the web interface*.

Use the following command to check your configuration.

```
# display local-user
```

Save your settings by using the command below.

```
# save
```

To delete an existing user account, enter the configuration mode and use the following command.

```
# undo local-user bill
```

Enabling Remote Access

After finishing the account management process, the network administrator needs to enable each one of the remote access services desired, therefore, open the web interface, select the *Network* menu and click on the *Service option* to be sent to the service management page.

On the service management page, you will be presented with six options of services available on the switch, as shown below.

Service	
▶FTP	☐ Enable FTP service
Telnet	☑ Enable Telnet service
SSH	☑ Enable SSH service
SFTP	☐ Enable SFTP service
▶HTTP	☑ Enable HTTP service
▶HTTPS	☑ Enable HTTPS service

To enable a service, select the desired check box and click on the *Apply* button.

In our example, the telnet, ssh, http and https were enabled.

As a good practice, the network administrator should try to keep a small number of services enabled and always opt for services that use data encryption, like ssh and https.

After finishing the service setup, be sure to save your settings by clicking on the *Save* option available at the top right of the screen.

In order to test your configuration, open the Putty software, as shown below.

ACCESS MANAGEMENT

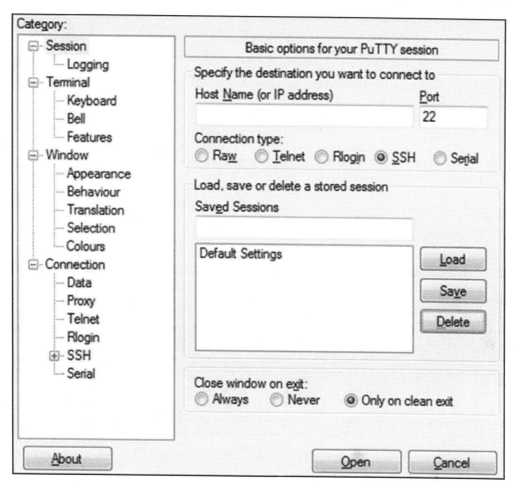

To test the telnet communication, on the Putty configuration screen, select the *telnet* connection type, enter the *IP address* of the remote switch and click on the *Apply* button.

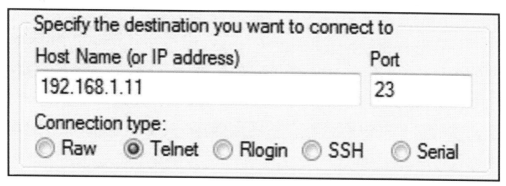

To test the *ssh* communication, on the Putty configuration screen, select the ssh connection type, enter the *IP address* of the remote switch and click on the *Apply* button.

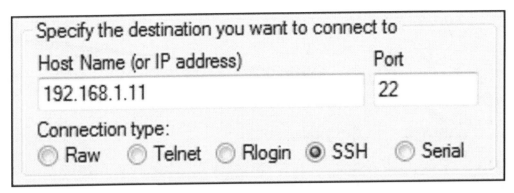

To test the http communication, open a browser, enter the **IP address** of the remote switch preceded by **http://** and try to access the web interface.

To test the https communication, open a browser, enter the **IP address** of the remote switch preceded by **https://** and try to access the web interface.

It is possible that some readers prefer to use the command-line instead of the web interface, therefore, we will also teach you how to enable a service using the command-line.

Using either the console, telnet or ssh, connect to the command-line of your switch and log in with a user who has administrative privileges.

If available to your switch model, enter the **_cmdline-mode** command in order to access the secret command-line mode of the device.

```
# _cmdline-mode on
```

Use the ***system-view*** command to enter the configuration mode.

```
# system-view
```

Use the following command to enable the telnet service.

```
# telnet server enable
```

Use the following command to disable the telnet service.

```
# undo telnet server enable
```

Use the following command to enable the ssh service.

ACCESS MANAGEMENT

```
# ssh server enable
```

Use the following command to check the status of ssh service.

```
# display ssh server status
```

Use the following command to disable the ssh service.

```
# undo ssh server enable
```

Configure the remote access interfaces to request the authentication by username and password.

```
# user-interface vty 0 15
# authentication-mode scheme
```

Use the following command to enable the http web interface service.

```
# ip http enable
```

Use the following command to check the status of the http service.

```
# display ip http
```

Use the following command to disable the http web interface service.

```
# undo ip http enable
```

Use the following command to enable the https web interface service.

```
# ip https enable
```

Use the following command to check the status of the https service.

```
# display ip https
```

Use the following command to disable the https web interface service.

```
# undo ip https enable
```

Save your settings by using the command below.

```
# save
```

Conclusion

This chapter taught using practical examples how to do the account management and how to enable the remote access services, in order to help the network administrator achieve better access control.

Throughout this chapter, we were able to follow Luke while he configured a network switch to meet the following project requirements listed in the document called ***requirements of the new network***.

- It must be possible to manage each switch remotely via telnet, ssh, and http
- It must be possible to use different access levels to the switches

At the end of this chapter, the reader should be able to improve teamwork by performing the creation of groups, users and enabling the remote access services.

To improve the learning curve, the following videos were published on our youtube channel showing how to use the techniques presented in this chapter:

- HP Switch – User Management
- HP Switch – How to configure Telnet
- HP Switch – How to configure SSH
- HP Switch – How to configure HTTPS

– Chapter 05 –

VIRTUAL NETWORK

After finishing the initial setup of the network switches, Luke decided to isolate the company's servers from the workstations through the use of vlans.

Information security certifications such as ISO 27001 require the implementation of access controls such as the segregation of the network based on groups of users or services to reduce the risk of unauthorized access to the network.

Virtual Network is an access control technique that allows the network administrator to logically isolate devices connected to a switch within a group.

This chapter will teach how to perform the vlan management through a detailed step by step approach.

Throughout this chapter, the following tasks related to the implementation of the network project will be presented:

• How to create a Vlan
• How to connect a device to a Vlan
• How to connect two switches using a Vlan trunk

All the lessons included in this chapter will be presented in a practical way using Luke's point of view during the implementation of his project.

Creating a Vlan

After a brief planning, it was decided that two groups of computers needed to be created in order to separate the company's servers and the workstations used by the employees.

In our example, computers that play a server role should be connected to the vlan 10, while the desktops and laptops used by employees should be connected to the vlan 20.

Open the web interface, select the **Network** menu and click on the **VLAN** option to be sent to the virtual network management page.

In order to create a new Vlan, select the **Create** tab, enter a numeric identifier for the virtual network and click on the **Create** button.

Network Project with HP Switch

| Select VLAN | Create | Port Detail | Detail | Modify VLAN | Modify Port | Remove |

Create:
VLAN IDs: [10]   Example:3, 5-10
                              Create

During the creation of a vlan you can set a description for the virtual network, therefore, select the vlan created earlier, type a brief description and click on the *Apply* button.

Modify VLAN description (Note: you can do this later on the Modify VLAN page)
  Modify the description of the selected VLAN:
  ID   Description
  1   [SERVERS]   (1-32 Chars.)
                                                        Apply

In our example, two vlans were created. The first vlan represent the company's servers and received the identification number 10, while the second vlan represent the company's workstations and received the identification number 20.

After finishing the vlan creation, be sure to save your settings by clicking on the *Save* option available at the top right of the screen.

If you need to remove an existing vlan, access the *Remove* tab, select the vlan desired and click on the *Remove* button.

It is possible that some readers prefer to use the command-line instead of the web interface, therefore, we will also teach you how to create a vlan using the command-line.

Using either the console, telnet or ssh, connect to the command-line of your switch and log in with a user who has administrative privileges.

If available to your switch model, enter the *_cmdline-mode* command in order to access the secret command-line mode of the device.

```
# _cmdline-mode on
```

Use the *system-view* command to enter the configuration mode.

```
# system-view
```

Create a vlan using the following commands.

```
# vlan 10
# description SERVERS
```

VIRTUAL NETWORK

```
# vlan 20
# description DESKTOP
# quit
```

Use the following command to check your configuration.

```
# display vlan
```

Save your settings by using the command below.

```
# save
```

To delete an existing vlan, enter the configuration mode and use the following command.

```
# undo vlan 10
```

Vlan Configuration

After finishing the vlan creation, we will show how to configure a switch port as a vlan member, therefore, open the web interface, select the *Network* menu and click on the *VLAN* option to be sent to the virtual network management page.

In order to configure a switch port as a vlan member, access the *Modify Port* tab, select the desired port, select the *Link type* option box, select the *Access* option on the combo box and click on the *Apply* button.

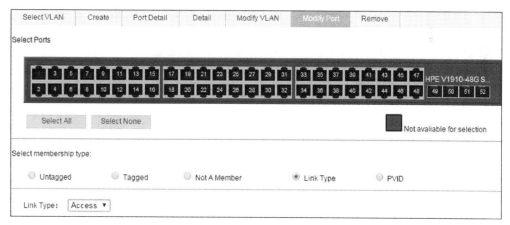

The access link type specifies that a switch port is a member of a single vlan, therefore, all devices connected to this port are automatically associated with the vlan without the need for any additional configuration on the end device itself.

Once the link type configuration is done, the network administrator needs to associate this switch port with a particular vlan, therefore, select the desired port, select the *Untagged* option box, enter the vlan identification number and click on the *Apply* button.

Network Project with HP Switch

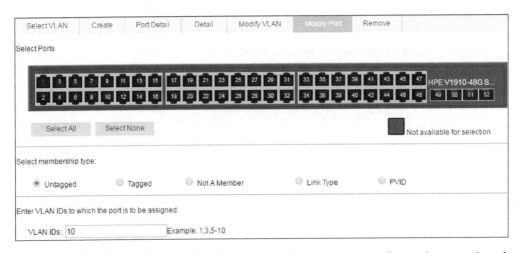

The *untagged* membership type specifies that no extra configuration need to be done on the end device connected to the switch port, and all the vlan tagging will be done by the network switch itself.

In our example, the first switch port was configured in access mode and was associated with the vlan 10, therefore, any device connected to this port will be a member to the server vlan.

To check your settings, access the *Port Detail* tab, select the desired port and verify if the information displayed is correct.

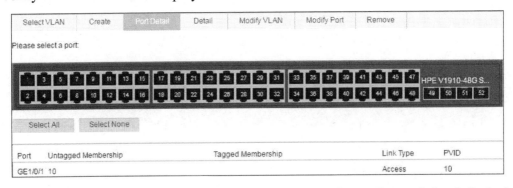

It is important to notice that if a switch port has not been changed, by default, it will be configured in access mode and as part of the default vlan 1.

After finishing the vlan management process, be sure to save your settings by clicking on the *Save* option available at the top right of the screen.

It is possible that some readers prefer to use the command-line instead of the web interface, therefore, we will also teach you how to configure a switch port as vlan member using the command-line.

Using either the console, telnet or ssh, connect to the command-line of your switch and log in with a user who has administrative privileges.

VIRTUAL NETWORK

If available to your switch model, enter the _cmdline-mode command in order to access the secret command-line mode of the device.

```
# _cmdline-mode on
```

Use the *system-view* command to enter the configuration mode.

```
# system-view
```

Configure the switch port in access mode and associate an existing vlan.

```
# interface GigabitEthernet1/0/1
# port link-type access
# port access vlan 10
```

Use the following command to check your configuration.

```
# display interface brief
```

Save your settings by using the command below.

```
# save
```

To remove a vlan association, enter the configuration mode and use the following command.

```
# interface GigabitEthernet1/0/1
# undo port link-type
# undo port access vlan
```

Trunk Configuration

After finishing the vlan creation, we will show how to configure a switch port as a trunk, therefore, open the web interface, select the *Network* menu and click on the *VLAN* option to be sent to the virtual network management page.

In order to configure a switch port in trunk mode, access the *Modify Port* tab, select the desired port, select the *Link type* option box, select the *Trunk* option on the combo box and click on the *Apply* button.

Network Project with HP Switch

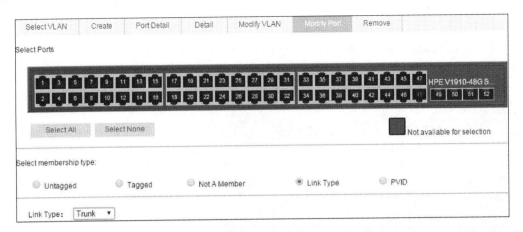

The ***trunk*** link type specifies that a port is able to send and receive traffic from multiple vlans, usually, this mode is used to connect two switches in order to allow communication between the devices that are on the same vlan but are physically connected to different switches.

Although the switch port was configured as a trunk, we still need to perform two extra configuration tasks in order to complete the setup.

First, the network administrator needs to configure a list of allowed vlans to pass through this switch port, therefore, select the desired port, select the ***Tagged*** option box, enter the identification number of authorized vlans separated by commas and click on the ***Apply*** button.

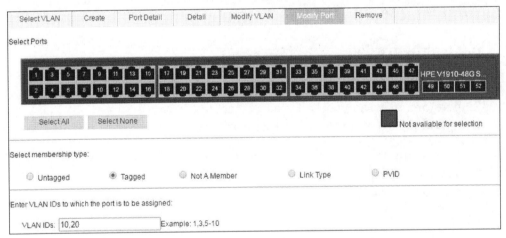

Second, the network administrator needs to configure a default vlan for the trunk, therefore, select the desired port, select the ***Untagged*** option box, enter the identification number of the desired default vlan and click on the ***Apply*** button.

VIRTUAL NETWORK

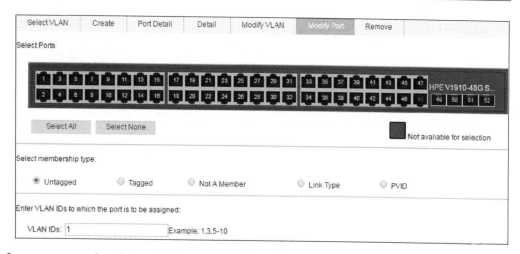

In our example, the switch port number 48 was configured in trunk mode, the traffic from the vlans 1, 10 and 20 were allowed and the vlan 1 was set as the default vlan for this trunk.

If the network switch receives a packet without a vlan identification on port 48, the device will *automatically assume* that this package is a member of the default vlan 1.

In order to function properly, the trunk port configured on **switch A** must be configured the same way as the trunk port of **switch B**. In our example, the port 48 of the switch *fkit-sw01* was configured the same way that the port 48 of the switch *fkit-sw02*.

To check your settings, access the **Port Detail** tab, select the desired port and verify if the information displayed is correct.

After finishing the trunk configuration, be sure to save your settings by clicking on the **Save** option available at the top right of the screen.

It is possible that some readers prefer to use the command-line instead of the web interface, therefore, we will also teach you how to configure a trunk using the command-line.

45

Network Project with HP Switch

Using either the console, telnet or ssh, connect to the command-line of your switch and log in with a user who has administrative privileges.

If available to your switch model, enter the *_cmdline-mode* command in order to access the secret command-line mode of the device.

```
# _cmdline-mode on
```

Use the *system-view* command to enter the configuration mode.

```
# system-view
```

Configure the switch port in trunk mode, set the default vlan and associate a list of allowed vlans.

```
# interface GigabitEthernet1/0/48
# port link-type trunk
# port trunk pvid vlan 1
# port trunk permit vlan 1 10 20
```

Use the following command to check your configuration.

```
# display port trunk
```

Save your settings by using the command below.

```
# save
```

To remove a trunk setup, enter the configuration mode and use the following command.

```
# interface GigabitEthernet1/0/48
# undo port link-type
```

Hybrid Configuration

A switch port in hybrid mode combines the characteristics of the access and trunk mode in order to allow traffic of multiple vlans, which *might be tagged or not*.

After assessing the requirements of the project, Luke came to the conclusion that in order to deploy the network project he will not need to use ports in hybrid mode, therefore, the following configuration will be demonstrated for educational purposes only.

In order to configure a switch port in hybrid mode, access the *Modify Port* tab, select the desired port, select the *Link type* option box, select the *Hybrid* option on the combo box and click on the *Apply* button.

VIRTUAL NETWORK

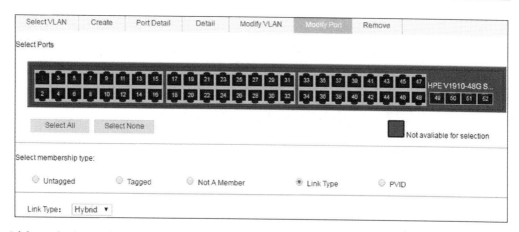

Although the switch port was configured as a hybrid, we still need to perform two extra configuration tasks in order to complete the setup.

First, the network administrator needs to configure a list of *tagged vlans* allowed to pass through this switch port, therefore, select the desired port, select the *Tagged* option box, enter the identification number of authorized vlans separated by commas and click on the *Apply* button.

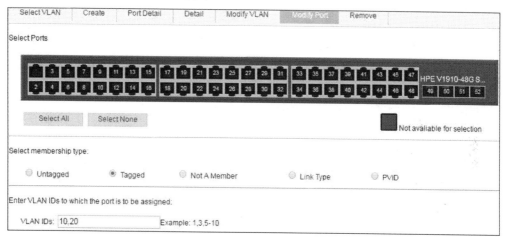

Second, the network administrator needs to configure a list of *untagged vlans* allowed to pass through this switch port, therefore, select the desired port, select the *Untagged* option box, enter the identification number of authorized vlans separated by commas and click on the *Apply* button.

47

Network Project with HP Switch

In our example, the switch port number 1 was configured in hybrid mode, the traffic from the vlans 1 and 2 was authorized without the tagging while the traffic of vlan 10 and 20 was authorized with tagging.

To check your settings, access the **Port Detail** tab, select the desired port and verify if the information displayed is correct.

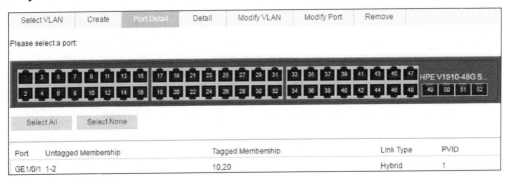

After finishing the hybrid port configuration, be sure to save your settings by clicking on the **Save** option available at the top right of the screen.

It is possible that some readers prefer to use the command-line instead of the web interface, therefore, we will also teach you how to configure a hybrid port using the command-line.

Using either the console, telnet or ssh, connect to the command-line of your switch and log in with a user who has administrative privileges.

If available to your switch model, enter the **_cmdline-mode** command in order to access the secret command-line mode of the device.

```
# _cmdline-mode on
```

Use the **system-view** command to enter the configuration mode.

```
# system-view
```

48

Configure the switch port in hybrid mode, set a list of tagged and untagged vlans allowed.

```
# interface GigabitEthernet1/0/1
# port link-type hybrid
# port hybrid vlan 10 20 tagged
# port hybrid vlan 1 2 untagged
```

Use the following command to check your configuration.

```
# display port hybrid
```

To prevent any configuration loss, save your settings by using the command below.

```
# save
```

To remove a hybrid port setup, enter the configuration mode and use the following command.

```
# interface GigabitEthernet1/0/1
# undo port link-type
```

Conclusion

This chapter taught using practical examples how to create and manage a vlan environment, in order to help the network administrator improve his control over the network.

Throughout this chapter, we were able to follow Luke while he configured a network switch to meet the following project requirements listed in the document called ***requirements of the new network***.

- The company's servers should be isolated in an exclusive vlan
- The company's workstations should be isolated in an exclusive vlan

At the end of this chapter, the reader should be able to create new vlans, configure a switch port as a vlan member and enable the communication between devices in the same vlan that are connected to different switches using a trunk.

To improve the learning curve, the following videos were published on our youtube channel showing how to use the techniques presented in this chapter:

- HP Switch – Vlan Configuration
- HP Switch – Trunk Configuration
- HP Switch – Hybrid Interface Configuration

– Chapter 06 –

ROUTING BETWEEN VLANS

Through the use of vlans, we are able to create a logical isolation between devices connected to the same switch, therefore, we can state that a workstation attached to the vlan 20 will not be able to communicate with a server connected to the vlan 10.

In order to enable the communication between devices connected in different vlans, the network administrator needs to perform the installation and configuration of a device with routing capability.

During the project planning phase, presented in the first chapter of this book, Luke assessed the stakeholder requirements and decided to purchase the switch models 1910 and A5500 to implement the network project.

Among the switches purchased for the project, the model A5500 was chosen as the main switch of the network and will be responsible for enabling routing between vlans.

Throughout this chapter, the following tasks related to the implementation of the network project will be presented:

- How to do the first access to a switch through the console
- How to do the first access to a switch through the web interface
- How to setup an IP address on a switch
- How to enable routing between vlans
- How to create a static default route
- How to install a Dhcp server

All the lessons included in this chapter will be presented in a practical way using Luke's point of view during the implementation of his project and the configuration of the main switch, ***model A5500.***

Initial Setup

The reader should be aware that there are several models of HP network switches, therefore, some of the initial setup steps shown in the second chapter of this book may not be applicable to the switch model A5500.

After finishing the physical connection between a computer and the console interface of the switch, the network administrator needs to use a specific software to access the command-line interface of the switch, therefore, visit the *putty.org* website and download *Putty*.

In order for the computer to be able to communicate with this switch model through a console cable you will need to customize the connection settings, therefore after opening *Putty*, select the category named *serial* and change the following parameters.

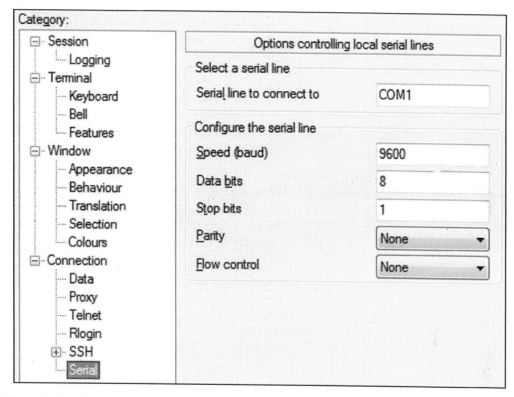

The *Serial line* option specifies which communication port that the computer should use to communicate with the network switch. In our example, it was decided that the computer should use the communication port COM1 to communicate with the switch.

Notice that the number of the communication port being used may vary, therefore, if the *com1* communication port does not work, try to use the next communication port *com2*, and so on.

The *Speed option* determines the transmission rate that should be used to communicate with the network switch. In our example, the speed was set to use a 9600 bits transmission rate as indicated by the product manual.

Notice that the manual of the network switch should be consulted because different switch models may require different connection speeds. In our example, while the switch model 1910 uses the communication speed of 38400 the A5500 model uses the speed of 9600.

The **Data bits** option specifies the amount of bits containing information that can be sent at once to the network switch. In our example, the option was set to use 8 bits, as indicated by the product manual.

The **Stop bits** option specifies the number of bits that should be used to signal a break or an end in the communication with the network switch. In our example, the option was set to use only a single bit, as indicated by the product manual.

The **Parity** option was formerly used to detect communication failures due to interference, but currently, this parameter is no longer used. In our example, it was determined that the parity should not be used.

The **Flow control** parameter was formerly used to set which flow control mechanism should be utilized but currently this parameter is no longer used. In our example, it was determined that the flow control should not be used.

After setting all the parameters of the serial connection as shown, go to the *session* category, select the **Serial** connection type option and click on the **Open** button to start the communication between the network switch and the computer.

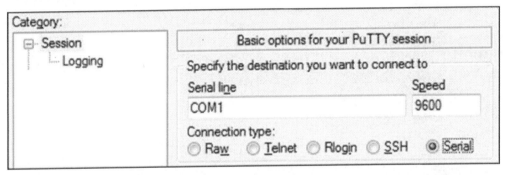

After clicking on the **Open** button, the following screen should be presented.

```
Startup configuration file does not exist.
It will take a long time to get configuration file, please wait...
Press CTRL_C to break

Retrieving configuration file failed!

User interface aux0 is available.
Press ENTER to get started.
```

In our example, it was shown how to perform the initial access to the command-line of a switch through its console interface using the software named Putty and a console cable.

It is important to highlight that, by default, this switch model will allow access to the console without requesting any authentication information, therefore, the network administrator needs to create a user account with administrative privileges and configure the console interface to request the authentication by username and password.

Use the *system-view* command to enter the configuration mode.

```
# system-view
```

Create a group of users with administrative permissions.

```
# user-group FKIT-ADMIN
# authorization-attribute level 3
```

Use the following command to check your configuration.

```
# display user-group
```

Create a user account with administrative permissions.

```
# local-user admin
# password simple kamisama123@
# group FKIT-ADMIN
# service-type terminal
# service-type ssh telnet
# service-type web
```

In our example, the username admin received the *management* access level and permission to connect to the switch using the *console, ssh, telnet and the web interface*.

Use the following command to check your configuration.

```
# display local-user
```

As a security measure, configure the console interface to request the authentication by username and password.

```
# user-interface aux 0
# authentication-mode scheme
```

In order to test the configuration, close your console session using the *quit* command and try to log in using the *admin* username and password previously created.

Setting an IP Address

During the initial setup phase of the switch, the network administrator will have to define an administrative IP address that will be used to access the equipment remotely.

Use the *system-view* command to enter the configuration mode.

53

Network Project with HP Switch

```
# system-view
```

Use the following commands to access the default interface *Vlan-interface1* and configure an administrative IP address.

```
# int Vlan-interface 1
# ip address 192.168.1.1 255.255.255.0
```

Use the following command to check your configuration.

```
# display interface Vlan-interface 1
```

In order to test the setup, you should configure an IP address of the same network on a computer and connect it into any port of the network switch.

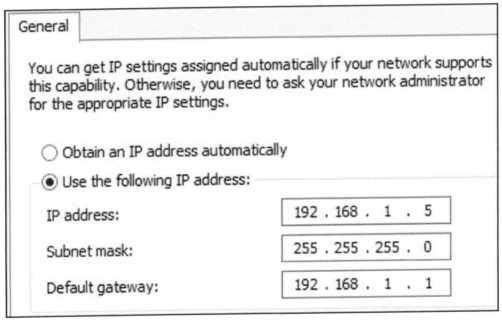

After connecting your computer to a switch port, access the command-line interface of your switch, quit the configuration mode and attempt a connectivity test between the computer and the switch using the *ping* command.

```
# quit
# ping 192.168.1.5
```

After finishing the configuration and the connectivity test between the devices successfully, use the *system-view* command to enter the configuration mode and enable the http web interface service on your switch.

```
# system-view
# ip http enable
```

54

After finishing the configuration and the connectivity test between the devices, open your browser, type the IP address of the network switch and access its web interface.

On the web interface initial login screen, enter the user account created, its password and enter the verification code displayed on the screen.

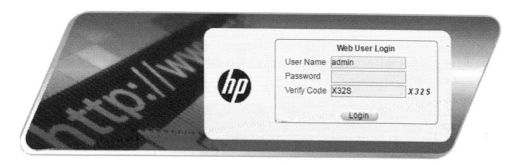

After a successful login, save the network switch settings by clicking on the *Save* option available at the top right of the screen.

In our example, we showed how to perform the configuration of an administrative IP address using the command-line interface; we also showed how to access the web interface and how to save the network switch configuration.

Device Types

After assessing the requirements of the project, Luke decided that four types of devices should be allowed to connect to the new network, therefore, here we present the list of devices and their descriptions.

The company's servers must be connected to vlan **10** and must be manually configured to use an IP address from the 192.168.**10**.0/24 network.

The company's workstations must be connected to vlan **20** and be automatically configured to use an IP address from the 192.168.**20**.0/24 network by the dhcp server.

The company's phones must be connected to vlan **30** and be automatically configured to use an IP address from the 192.168.**30**.0/24 network by the dhcp server.

The external visitors' computers must be connected to vlan **40** and be automatically configured to use an IP address from the 192.168.**40**.0/24 network by the dhcp server.

Step by Step Guide

The process of routing between vlans is complex and requires full attention from the network administrator in order to understand and perform the many steps required.

As the first step, the network administrator needs to access the main network switch and create each one of the vlans being connected through routing.

As the second step, the network administrator needs to access the main network switch and create a virtual vlan interface for each one of the vlans being connected through routing.

As the third step, the network administrator needs to access the main network switch and create a static default route, in order to connect the internal network devices to the internet.

As the fourth step, the network administrator needs to access the main network switch and configure the dhcp service, in order to assign IP addresses automatically to devices connected to the desktop, visitor and phone vlans.

Vlan Creation

As the first step, the network administrator needs to create all the required vlans on the main network switch.

Open the web interface, select the *Network* menu and click on the *VLAN* option to be sent to the virtual network management page.

To create multiple vlans, select the *Create* tab, enter the identification numbers separated by commas and click on the *Create* button.

During the creation of a vlan you can set a description for your virtual network, therefore, select a vlan created earlier, type a brief description and click on the *Apply* button.

ROUTING BETWEEN VLANS

```
Modify VLAN description (Note: you can do this later on the Modify VLAN page)
    Modify the description of the selected VLAN:
    ID          Description
    1           SERVERS                              (1-32 Chars.)
                                                          Apply
```

In our example, all the necessary vlans for project implementation were created and received their respective descriptions.

It is possible that some readers prefer to use the command-line instead of the web interface, therefore, we will also teach you how to create a vlan using the command-line.

Using either the console, telnet or ssh, connect to the command-line of your switch and log in with a user who has administrative privileges.

Use the *system-view* command to enter the configuration mode.

```
# system-view
```

Create the required vlans using the following commands.

```
# vlan 10
# description SERVERS

# vlan 20
# description DESKTOP

#vlan 30
# description VOIP

# vlan 40
# description GUESTS
# quit
```

Use the following command to check your configuration.

```
# display vlan
```

Save your settings by using the command below.

```
# save
```

Virtual Interface Creation

As the second step, the network administrator needs to create a virtual vlan interface for each one of the vlans being connected through routing.

In the past, if you wanted to enable routing between two networks, a routing device with two physical interfaces had to be used, and each interface had to be connected to a different network.

Nowadays, the use of physical interfaces is not a must, and a network administrator can use virtual network interfaces to perform the same function.

In our example, the main switch will perform the routing between the vlans of the network project through the use of virtual interfaces.

After finishing the vlan creation, open the web interface, select the *Network* menu and click on the *VLAN Interface* option to be sent to the virtual interface management page.

To create a virtual interface, access the *Create* tab, select the option to *Configure an IPv4 address*, uncheck the *Configure IPv6 link-local address* option, enter the identifier of an existing vlan, select the *Manual* setup option, enter the desired IP address, the network mask and click on the *Apply* button.

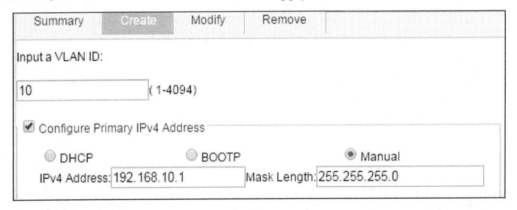

After finish creating the first virtual interface, repeat the process for all the vlans involved in the project. In our example, the virtual interfaces 10, 20, 30 and 40 were created.

In our example, the virtual interface *VLAN-Interface10* was created, configured with the 192.168.**10.1** IP address and the 255.255.255.0 network mask.

In our example, the virtual interface *VLAN-interface20* was created, configured with the 192.168.**20.1** IP address and the 255.255.255.0 network mask.

In our example, the virtual interface *VLAN-interface30* was created, configured with the 192.168.**30.1** IP address and the 255.255.255.0 network mask.

In our example, the virtual interface *VLAN-interface40* was created, configured with the 192.168.**40.1** IP address and the 255.255.255.0 network mask.

ROUTING BETWEEN VLANS

It is possible that some readers prefer to use the command-line instead of the web interface, therefore, we will also teach you how to create a virtual interface using the command-line.

Using either the console, telnet or ssh, connect to the command-line of your switch and log in with a user who has administrative privileges.

Use the *system-view* command to enter the configuration mode.

```
# system-view
```

Create the required virtual interfaces using the following commands.

```
# interface Vlan-interface10
# ip address 192.168.10.1 255.255.255.0
# undo shutdown

# interface Vlan-interface20
# ip address 192.168.20.1 255.255.255.0
# undo shutdown

# interface Vlan-interface30
# ip address 192.168.30.1 255.255.255.0
# undo shutdown

# interface Vlan-interface40
# ip address 192.168.40.1 255.255.255.0
# undo shutdown
```

Use the following command to check your configuration.

```
# display interface Vlan-interface 10

Vlan-interface10 current state: UP
Line protocol current state: UP
```

In order for the routing between vlans to work correctly all the virtual interfaces involved in the process should be up and running as shown above, i.e., *up/up*.

It is possible that a virtual interface remains offline in case the network switch does not have at least one port associated with this vlan.

It is possible that a virtual interface remains offline in case the network switch does not have at least one port configured in trunk mode allowing the passage of this vlan.

After finishing the configuration of all virtual interfaces and make sure that all virtual interfaces are up and running, we can state that the routing between vlans was successfully configured.

59

In our example, the network administrator performed the creation and configuration of 4 virtual interfaces in order to enable routing between these networks.

Setting the Default Route

As the third step, the network administrator needs to create a default route on the main network switch, in order to connect the internal network devices to the internet through the company's firewall.

Open the web interface, access the *Network* menu and click on the *IPV4 Routing* option to be sent to the route management page.

In order to create a new route, access the *Create* tab, enter the network address, its network mask and click on the *Apply* button.

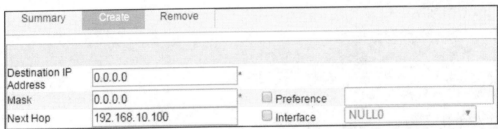

In our example, a static default route was created pointing to the company's firewall IP address 192.168.10.100 as the default gateway.

It is possible that some readers prefer to use the command-line instead of the web interface, therefore, we will also teach you how to create a static default route using the command-line.

Using either the console, telnet or ssh, connect to the command-line of your switch and log in with a user who has administrative privileges.

Use the *system-view* command to enter the configuration mode.

```
# system-view
```

Use the *ip* command to create a default static route.

```
# ip route-static 0.0.0.0 0.0.0.0 192.168.10.100
```

Use the following command to check your configuration.

```
# display ip routing-table
```

Save your settings by using the command below.

```
# save
```

DHCP Server Installation

As the fourth step, the network administrator needs to install a dhcp server in order to assign IP addresses automatically to devices connected to the desktop, visitor and phone vlans.

Open the web interface, access the **Network** menu and click on the **DHCP** option to be sent to the service setup screen.

To enable dhcp service globally, access the **DHCP Server** tab, select the **Enable** option and click on the **Apply** button.

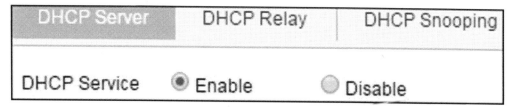

After enabling dhcp service globally, select the **Dynamic** option, click on the **Add** button in order to add a new network to the dhcp server and set the other configuration options, as shown below.

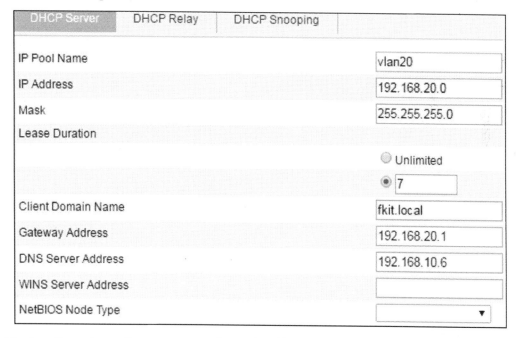

During the setup of a new network on the dhcp server, the network administrator will need to set a number of service parameters, therefore, here we present a list of parameters and their descriptions.

61

The **IP pool name** parameter specifies a scope name to identify the new network being added to the dhcp server. In our example, we configured the vlan20 word as the scope identification.

The **IP address** parameter specifies a new network being added to the dhcp server. In our example, the vlan20 scope was configured to assign the 192.168.20.0 network through the dhcp server.

The **Mask** parameter specifies which network mask should be offered through this dhcp server scope. In our example, the vlan20 scope was configured to assign the 255.255.255.0 network mask.

The **Lease duration** parameter specifies the duration of the address lease offered through this dhcp server scope. In our example, the vlan20 scope was configured to lease an IP address for seven days.

The **Client domain** parameter specifies which dns domain should be offered through this dhcp server scope. In our example, the vlan20 scope was configured to assign the fkit.local domain name.

The **Gateway address** parameter specifies which default gateway IP address should be offered through this dhcp server scope. In our example, the vlan20 scope was configured to assign 192.168.20.1 as its default gateway.

The **DNS Server Address** parameter specifies which dns servers should be offered through this dhcp server scope. In our example, the vlan20 scope was configured to assign the 192.168.10.6 dns server.

After finishing the configuration of all parameters, replicate the scope creation process for all vlans that should receive automatically IP address allocation through the dhcp server. In our example, this process was replicated to the 30 and 40 vlans.

In our example, if a computer is connected to a switch port that is member of *vlan 20* it will automatically receive an IP address from the *192.168.20.0* network with the *255.255.255.0* network mask, its default gateway will be set as *192.168.20.1*, its dns domain will be set as *fkit.local*, its dns server will be set as *192.168.10.6* and all these settings will be valid for *7 days*.

In our example, if a computer is connected to a switch port that is member of *vlan 30* it will automatically receive an IP address from the *192.168.30.0* network with the *255.255.255.0* network mask, its default gateway will be set as *192.168.30.1*, its dns domain will be set as *fkit.local*, its dns server will be set as *192.168.10.6* and all these settings will be valid for *7 days*.

In our example, if a computer is connected to a switch port that is member of *vlan 40* it will automatically receive an IP address from the *192.168.40.0* network with the *255.255.255.0* network mask, its default gateway will be set as *192.168.40.1*, its dns domain will be set as *fkit.local*, its dns server will be set as *192.168.10.6* and all these settings will be valid for *7 days*.

It is possible that some readers prefer to use the command-line instead of the web interface, therefore, we will also teach you how to setup a dhcp server using the command-line.

Using either the console, telnet or ssh, connect to the command-line of your switch and log in with a user who has administrative privileges.

Use the *system-view* command to enter the configuration mode.

```
# system-view
```

Enable dhcp service globally through command below.

```
# dhcp enable
```

Configure a dhcp scope named vlan20.

```
# dhcp server ip-pool vlan20
# network 192.168.20.0 mask 255.255.255.0
# gateway-list 192.168.20.1
# dns-list 192.168.10.6
# domain-name fkit.local
# expired day 7
```

Configure a dhcp scope named vlan30.

```
# dhcp server ip-pool vlan30
# network 192.168.30.0 mask 255.255.255.0
# gateway-list 192.168.30.1
# dns-list 192.168.10.6
# domain-name fkit.local
# expired day 7
```

Configure a dhcp scope named vlan40.

```
# dhcp server ip-pool vlan40
# network 192.168.40.0 mask 255.255.255.0
# gateway-list 192.168.40.1
# dns-list 192.168.10.6
# domain-name fkit.local
# expired day 7
```

Use the following command to check your dhcp scope configuration.

```
# display dhcp server tree pool vlan20
```

Use the following command to check the addresses leased by the dhcp server.

```
# display dhcp server ip-in-use all
```

Save your settings by using the command below.

```
# save
```

Conclusion

This chapter taught using practical examples how to perform routing between vlans and how to setup a dhcp server on the main network switch, in order to help the network administrator improve his control over the network.

Throughout this chapter, we were able to follow Luke while he configured the main network switch to meet the following project requirements listed in the document called ***requirements of the new network***.

- A switch should be elected as the main network switch
- The main network switch must provide routing between vlans
- The main network switch must be configured as dhcp server
- The company's workstations must receive the IP address from a dhcp server
- The company's phones must receive the IP address from a dhcp server
- External visitors must receive the IP address from a dhcp server

At the end of this chapter, the reader should be able to configure routing between vlans and perform the installation of a dhcp server.

To improve the learning curve, the following videos were published on our youtube channel showing how to use the techniques presented in this chapter:

- HP Switch – A5500 Initial IP Configuration
- HP Switch – Routing between Vlans
- HP Switch – Setting a Default Route
- HP Switch – Virtual Interface Creation
- HP Switch – DHCP Server Installation
- HP Switch – Using DHCP Relay

– Chapter 07 –

VOICE OVER IP

After finishing the setup of the main network switch, Luke decides it's time to perform voice over IP integration to the network.

Being a sensitive traffic, voice packets should be treated with higher priority by the switch, therefore, Luke decided to create an exclusive vlan to voice traffic.

This chapter will teach how to create and configure a voice vlan on a network switch through a detailed step by step approach.

Throughout this chapter, the following tasks related to the implementation of the network project will be presented:

• How to create a voice vlan
• How to connect a VoIP phone on a voice vlan

All the lessons included in this chapter will be presented in a practical way using Luke's point of view during the implementation of his project.

Creating a Voice Vlan

After a brief planning, it was decided that a voice exclusive vlan should be created in order to separate the voice traffic from the rest of the company's network traffic.

In our example, VoIP phones must be connected to the vlan 30, in order to separate the voice traffic from the data traffic generated by the workstations and servers network.

Open the web interface, select the *Network* menu and click on the *VLAN* option to be sent to the virtual network management page.

In order to create a new Vlan, select the *Create* tab, enter a numeric identifier for the virtual network and click on the *Create* button.

During the creation of a vlan you can set a description for the virtual network, therefore, select the vlan created earlier, type a brief description and click on the *Apply* button.

```
Modify VLAN description (Note: you can do this later on the Modify VLAN page)
    Modify the description of the selected VLAN:
    ID              Description
    30              VLAN 30 - VOIP                              (1-32 Chars.)
```

In our example, a vlan was created using the 30 identification number and a custom description.

After finishing the vlan management process, be sure to save your settings by clicking on the *Save* option available at the top right of the screen.

It is possible that some readers prefer to use the command-line instead of the web interface, therefore, we will also teach you how to create a vlan using the command-line.

Using either the console, telnet or ssh, connect to the command-line of your switch and log in with a user who has administrative privileges.

If available to your switch model, enter the *_cmdline-mode* command in order to access the secret command-line mode of the device.

```
# _cmdline-mode on
```

Use the *system-view* command to enter the configuration mode.

```
# system-view
```

Create a vlan using the following commands.

```
# vlan 30
# description VOIP
# quit
```

Use the following command to check your configuration.

```
# display vlan
```

Save your settings by using the command below.

```
# save
```

To delete an existing vlan, enter the configuration mode and use the following command.

```
# undo vlan 30
```

Voice Vlan Configuration

After a meeting with the stakeholders about the network topology, it was decided that only one switch port would be made available for each employee, therefore, if an employee needs to have two devices connected to the network these devices will have to share the same switch port.

If you need to share a physical port, the voip phone needs to be connected directly to the switch port while the workstation needs to be connected to an additional port of the phone.

It is important to highlight that a VoIP phone usually have two network interfaces, therefore, the external phone interface needs to be connected to a switch port while the internal phone interface needs to be attached to a workstation.

Due to the sharing, the switch port should be able to transmit the traffic of two vlans which are the desktop and phone vlans, therefore, the network administrator needs to configure this switch port as a trunk.

In our example, a switch port will be configured as a trunk in order to connect a phone and a workstation to the network.

Keep in mind that each device will have to be associated to the correct vlan automatically, therefore, the phones should be linked to the vlan 30 while the workstations should be associated with the vlan 20.

In order to configure the vlan automatically on the phone both the switch and the phone must support the *lldp* protocol.

To enable the LLDP protocol support on a VoIP phone, access the phone setup menu and enable the protocol according to the instructions listed in the *device manual*.

Regarding the switch, open the web interface, access the *Network* menu and click on the *LLDP* option to be sent to the protocol setup screen.

In order to enable the lldp protocol support, access the *Global Setup* tab, select the *Enable* lldp option and click on the *Apply* button.

Network Project with HP Switch

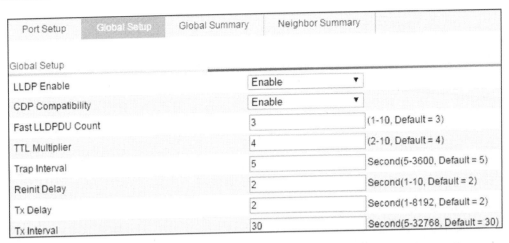

After enabling the LLDP protocol on both devices, go to the *Neighbor Summary* tab and check if the phone was detected by the switch using the lldp protocol.

In our example, the network switch detected a VoIP phone connected to the port 17 with the mac address 0004-f24e-21b9.

After finishing the lldp configuration, select the *Network* menu and click on the *VLAN* option to be sent to the virtual network management page.

In order to configure a switch port in trunk mode, access the *Modify Port* tab, select the desired port, select the *Link type* option box, select the *Trunk* option on the combo box and click on the *Apply* button.

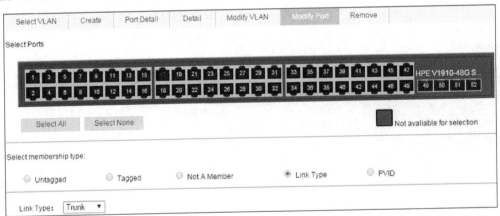

This port needs to be able to transfer traffic from two vlans, therefore, it should be configured in trunk mode in order to allow the traffic from the Desktop vlan and the VoIP vlan.

As the next step, we need to authorize the desktop vlan through the switch port in a transparent manner, therefore, select the desired port, select the *Untagged* option box, enter the identification number of the desktop vlan and click on the *Apply* button.

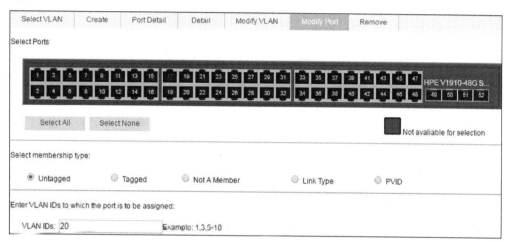

In our example, the switch port 17 was configured in trunk mode, the traffic from the vlan 20 was allowed and set as the default vlan for this trunk.

If the network switch receives a packet without a vlan identification on port 17, the device will ***automatically assume*** that this packet is a member of the default vlan 20.

At the moment, it is not necessary to add the voice vlan as one of the allowed vlans on the trunk because this setting will be done later.

After finishing the trunk configuration, access the *Network* menu and click on the *Voice VLAN* option to be sent to the voice vlan configuration screen.

Access the *Setup* tab and disable the feature called *Voice VLAN Security*.

Access the *Port Setup* tab, select the desired port, choose the *automatic* voice vlan mode, *enable* the voice vlan port state, enter the voice vlan identification number and click on the *Apply* button.

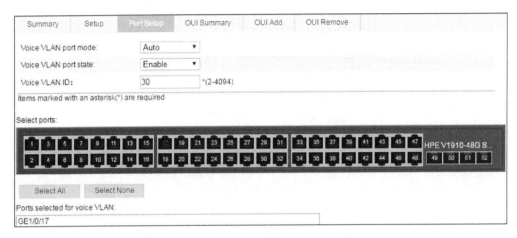

After finishing this task, the voice vlan will be added to the list of allowed vlans configured on the trunk.

As the last step, we need to register the device OUI address on the switch in order to *automatically* assign the phone to the voice vlan through the LLDP protocol.

If the OUI address of the manufacturer is not added to the switch database, all voip phones will need to have the vlan configuration done manually on each device.

OUI is the first six digits of the Mac address of a network device and identifies the manufacturer address; this information can be seen in the *Neighbor Summary* tab of the *LLDP* menu.

In our example, the switch detected a phone using the *0004-f24e-21b9* mac address connected to port 17, therefore, the phone's OUI address is *0004f2*.

After getting the OUI address, access the *OUI Add* tab, click on the *Add* button, enter the OUI address using the *ffff-ff00-0000* mask and a brief description.

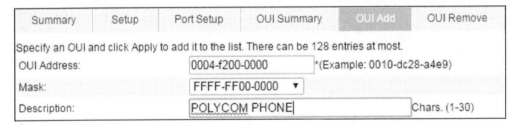

In our example, the network administrator added the *0004-f2000000* OUI address with the *FFFF-FF00-0000* mask and the *Polycom phone* description.

In our example, the switch port number 17 was configured in trunk mode, the traffic from vlans 20 and 30 were allowed as they correspond to the Desktop and Voice Vlan.

VOICE OVER IP

To check your settings, access the ***Summary*** tab and verify if the information displayed is correct.

Summary	Setup	Port Setup	OUI Summary	OUI Add	OUI Remove
Voice VLAN security:			Disabled		
Voice VLAN aging time:			1440 minutes		
Maximum of voice VLANs:			1		
Current number of voice VLANs:			1		

Ports enabled for voice VLAN:

Port Name	Voice VLAN ID	Mode
GigabitEthernet1/0/17	100	Auto

After finishing the voice vlan setup, be sure to save your settings by clicking on the ***Save*** option available at the top right of the screen.

It is possible that some readers prefer to use the command-line instead of the web interface, therefore, we will also teach you how to setup a voice vlan using the command-line.

Using either the console, telnet or ssh, connect to the command-line of your switch and log in with a user who has administrative privileges.

If available to your switch model, enter the **_cmdline-mode** command in order to access the secret command-line mode of the device.

```
# _cmdline-mode on
```

Use the ***system-view*** command to enter the configuration mode.

```
# system-view
```

Enable the lldp protocol support and optionally the cdp protocol compatibility.

```
# lldp enable
# lldp compliance cdp
```

As a requirement, the phone must have the lldp protocol enabled, therefore, access the phone setup menu and enable the protocol according to the instructions listed in the device manual.

After enabling the LLDP protocol on both devices, use the command below to check if the phone was detected by the switch using the lldp protocol.

```
# display lldp neighbor-information interface GigabitEthernet1/0/17 brief
```

In our example, the network switch encountered a phone connected to the switch port 17 using the 0004-f24e-21b9 mac address.

```
LLDP neighbor-information of port 17[GigabitEthernet1/0/17]:
  Neighbor 4:
    PortID/subtype    : 0004-f24e-21b9/MAC address
    Capabilities      : Bridge,Telephone
```

After getting the MAC address of the phone, add the OUI address using the ffff-ff00-0000 mask and a description to the network switch database.

```
# voice vlan mac-address 0004-f200-0000 mask ffff-ff00-0000 description POLYCOM PHONE
```

The command above allow all the phones that have the mac address beginning with 0004-f to have their vlan configured automatically.

Disable the voice vlan security mode.

```
# undo voice vlan security enable
```

Configure the switch port in trunk mode and set the desktop vlan as the default vlan.

```
# interface GigabitEthernet1/0/17
# port link-type trunk
# port trunk pvid vlan 20
# port trunk permit vlan 20
```

Enable the voice vlan feature and set the voice vlan identification.

```
# interface GigabitEthernet1/0/17
# voice vlan 30 enable
```

Use the following command to check your configuration.

```
# display voice vlan oui
# display voice vlan state
```

Save your settings by using the command below.

```
# save
```

To remove a voice vlan setup, enter the configuration mode and use the following command.

```
# interface GigabitEthernet1/0/17
# undo voice vlan enable
```

Conclusion

This chapter taught using practical examples how to create and manage a voice vlan environment, in order to help the network administrator improve his control over the network and the voice packets performance.

Throughout this chapter, we were able to follow Luke while he configured a network switch to meet the following project requirements listed in the document called ***requirements of the new network***.

• The company's phones should be isolated in an exclusive vlan
• A VoIP phone must have its voice vlan automatically configured
• A VoIP phone must be able to connect a desktop to the network

At the end of this chapter, the reader should be able to create a voice vlan, configure the communication between the switch and a phone using a trunk.

To improve the learning curve, the following video were published on our youtube channel showing how to use the techniques presented in this chapter:

• HP Switch – Voice Vlan Configuration

– Chapter 08 –

PERFORMANCE & REDUNDANCY

After finishing the core setup of the network switches, Luke decided to improve the performance and redundancy between devices through the use of link aggregation.

Link Aggregation is a generic term that defines the logical grouping of two or more physical network interfaces in order to provide network redundancy and improve the performance by combining the bandwidth of multiple interfaces.

As a performance example, the grouping of two Gigabit network interfaces on a switch would create one virtual interface with the accumulated bandwidth of 2 gigabits.

As a redundancy example, the virtual interface would continue to operate even if one of the physical interfaces stop working.

This chapter will teach how to perform multiple link aggregation configurations through a detailed step by step approach.

Throughout this chapter, the following tasks related to the implementation of the network project will be presented:

• How to configure link aggregation in trunk mode
• How to configure link aggregation in access mode

All the lessons included in this chapter will be presented in a practical way using Luke's point of view during the implementation of his project.

Link Aggregation – Trunk Mode

After analyzing the network project requirements, it was decided that any trunk connection between switches should use aggregated links, in order to improve the performance and offer a level of redundancy.

In our example, the network administrator will configure two switches to be connected using the link aggregation feature in trunk mode.

Open the web interface, select the **Network** menu and click on the **Link Aggregation** option to be sent to the link aggregation management page.

In order to create a new link aggregation, select the **Create** tab, enter a numeric identifier to the virtual interface, select the **Dynamic** option to enable the lacp

PERFORMANCE & REDUNDANCY

protocol utilization, select the *physical interfaces* that should be members of this group and click on the *Apply* button.

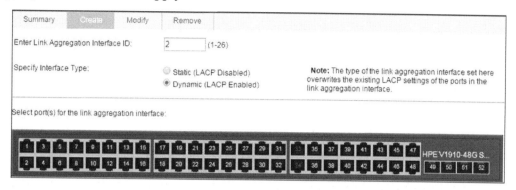

After clicking on the apply button, the network switch will create a new link aggregation interface using the group number entered as its identification number. In our example, the *Bridge-Aggregation2* virtual interface was created with the physical interfaces 33 and 34 as its members.

After finishing the virtual interface creation, you need to configure it like any other switch interface, therefore, access the *Network* menu and click on the *Vlan* option to be sent to the virtual network management page.

In order to configure the virtual interface in trunk mode, access the *Modify Port* tab, select the desired virtual interface on the Aggregation ports list, select the *Link type* option box, select the *Trunk* option on the combo box and click on the *Apply* button.

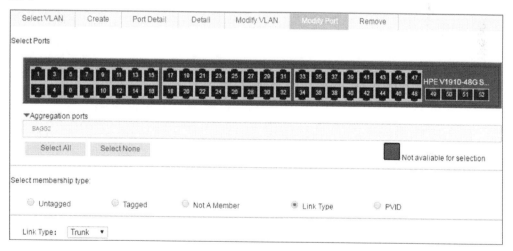

The *trunk* link type determines that a port is able to send and receive traffic from multiple vlans, usually, this mode is used to connect two switches in order to allow communication between the devices that are on the same vlan but are physically connected to different switches.

75

Although the switch port was configured as a trunk, we still need to perform two extra configuration tasks in order to complete the setup.

First, the network administrator needs to associate a list of allowed vlans to pass through this switch port, therefore, select the desired virtual interface, select the **Tagged** option box, enter the identification number of authorized vlans separated by commas and click on the **Apply** button.

Second, the network administrator needs to set a default vlan for the trunk, therefore, select the virtual interface, select the **Untagged** option box, enter the identification number of the desired default vlan and click on the **Apply** button.

In our example, the virtual interface **bagg2** was configured in trunk mode, the traffic from the vlans 1, 10 and 20 were allowed and the vlan 1 was set as the default vlan for this trunk.

PERFORMANCE & REDUNDANCY

To check your settings, access the ***Port Detail*** tab, select both the virtual interface and the physical interfaces to verify if the information displayed is correct.

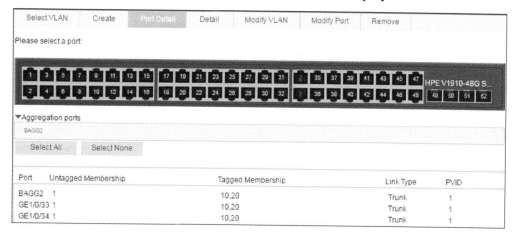

It is important to notice that all the configuration done to the virtual interface is automatically replicated to the physical interfaces that are members of the group.

After physically connecting the switches, access the ***Network*** menu, click on the ***Link aggregation*** option, select the ***Summary*** tab and check the status of your link aggregation.

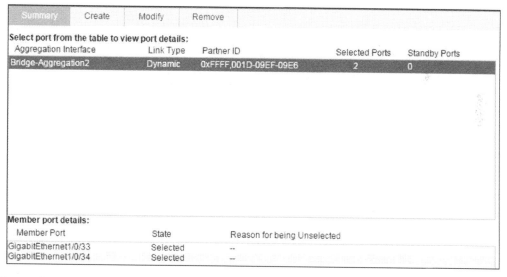

For safety reasons, the physical connection between two network switches should be performed only after both devices have been configured to use link aggregation.

After finishing the link aggregation setup, be sure to save your settings by clicking on the ***Save*** option available at the top right of the screen.

It is possible that some readers prefer to use the command-line instead of the web interface, therefore, we will also teach you how to setup a link aggregation in trunk mode using the command-line.

Using either the console, telnet or ssh, connect to the command-line of your switch and log in with a user who has administrative privileges.

If available to your switch model, enter the *cmdline-mode* command in order to access the secret command-line mode of the device.

```
# _cmdline-mode on
```

Use the *system-view* command to enter the configuration mode.

```
# system-view
```

Create a new link aggregation virtual interface and set the dynamic configuration mode in order to enable the use of the lacp protocol.

```
# interface Bridge-Aggregation2
# link-aggregation mode dynamic
# quit
```

Configure the physical interfaces 33 and 34 as members of the virtual interface Bridge-Aggregation2.

```
# interface GigabitEthernet1/0/33
# port link-aggregation group 2

# interface GigabitEthernet1/0/34
# port link-aggregation group 2
```

Configure the virtual link aggregation interface in trunk mode, set vlan 1 as the default vlan and allow the traffic from vlans 1, 10 and 20.

```
# interface Bridge-Aggregation2
# port link-type trunk
# port trunk pvid vlan 1
# port trunk permit vlan 1 10 20
```

Use the following command to check your configuration.

```
# display link-aggregation verbose
```

Save your settings by using the command below.

```
# save
```

To remove an existing link aggregation configuration, enter the configuration mode and use the following command.

```
# undo interface Bridge-Aggregation 2
```

Link Aggregation – Access Mode

After finishing a brief risk analysis, it was decided that the file server must have a redundant network connection in order to prevent the stoppage of the service which could lead to a high financial impact over the company.

In our example, the file server running Windows 2012 will be connected to the new network using the link aggregation feature in access mode.

Open the web interface, select the *Network* menu and click on the *Link aggregation* option to be sent to the link aggregation management page.

In order to create a new link aggregation, select the *Create* tab, enter a numeric identifier to the virtual interface, select the *Dynamic* option to enable the lacp protocol utilization, select the *physical interfaces* that should be members of this group and click on the *Apply* button.

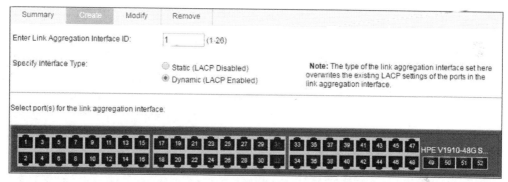

After clicking on the apply button, the network switch will create a new link aggregation interface using the group number entered as its identification number. In our example, the *Bridge-Aggregation1* virtual interface was created with the physical interfaces 31 and 32 as its members.

After finishing the virtual interface creation, you need to configure it like any other switch interface, therefore, access the *Network* menu and click on the *Vlan* option to be sent to the virtual network management page.

In order to configure the virtual interface in access mode, access the *Modify Port* tab, select the desired virtual interface, select the *Link type* option box, select the *Access* option on the combo box and click on the *Apply* button.

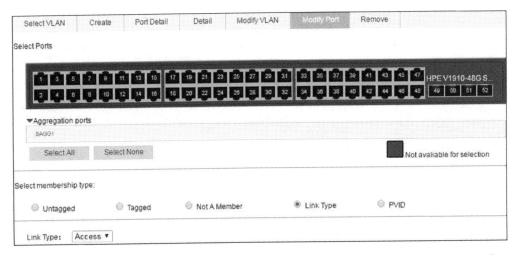

The access link type determines that a port is a member of a single vlan, therefore, all devices connected to this port are automatically associated with the vlan without the need for any additional configuration on the device itself.

Once the link type configuration is done, the network administrator needs to associate this switch port with a specific vlan, therefore, select the desired virtual interface, select the *Untagged* option box, enter the vlan identification number to which the interface should be associated and click on the *Apply* button.

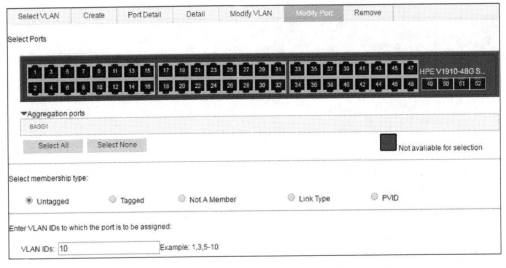

In our example, the virtual interface bagg1 was configured in access mode and was associated with the vlan 10, therefore, any device connected to this interface will be a member to the server vlan.

To check your settings, access the *Port Detail* tab, select both the virtual interface and the physical interfaces to verify if the information displayed is correct.

PERFORMANCE & REDUNDANCY

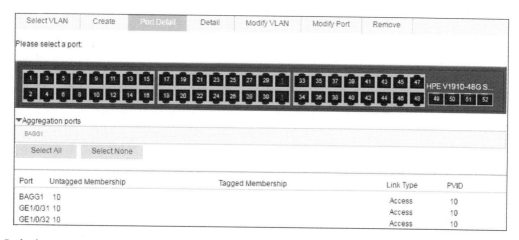

It is important to notice that all the configuration done to the virtual interface is automatically replicated to the physical interfaces that are members of the group.

After physically connecting the switches, access the *Network* menu, click on the *Link aggregation* option, select the *Summary* tab and check the status of your link aggregation.

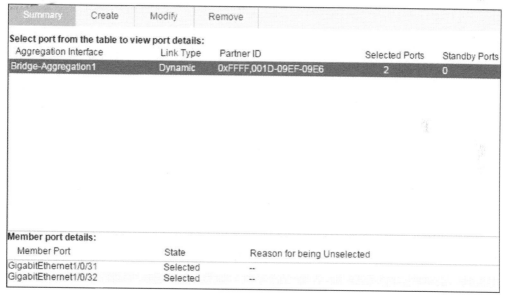

For safety reasons, the physical connection between the switch and the file server should be performed only after both devices have been configured to use link aggregation.

At the end of this chapter, there will be a step by step procedure showing how to configure a link aggregation on a computer running Windows 2012.

After finishing the link aggregation setup, be sure to save your settings by clicking on the *Save* option available at the top right of the screen.

It is possible that some readers prefer to use the command-line instead of the web interface, therefore, we will also teach you how to setup a link aggregation in access mode using the command-line.

Using either the console, telnet or ssh, connect to the command-line of your switch and log in with a user who has administrative privileges.

If available to your switch model, enter the *_cmdline-mode* command in order to access the secret command-line mode of the device.

```
# _cmdline-mode on
```

Use the *system-view* command to enter the configuration mode.

```
# system-view
```

Create a new link aggregation virtual interface and set the dynamic configuration mode in order to enable the use of the lacp protocol.

```
# interface Bridge-Aggregation1
# link-aggregation mode dynamic
# quit
```

Configure the physical interfaces 31 and 32 as members of the virtual interface Bridge-Aggregation1.

```
# interface GigabitEthernet1/0/31
# port link-aggregation group 1
# interface GigabitEthernet1/0/32
# port link-aggregation group 1
```

Configure the virtual link aggregation interface in access mode and associate the desired vlan.

```
# interface Bridge-Aggregation1
# port link-type access
# port access vlan 10
```

Use the following command to check your configuration.

```
# display link-aggregation verbose
```

Save your settings by using the command below.

```
# save
```

To remove an existing link aggregation configuration, enter the configuration mode and use the following command.

```
# undo interface Bridge-Aggregation 1
```

Link Aggregation – Windows 2012

After finishing a brief risk analysis, it was decided that the file server must have a redundant network connection in order to prevent the stoppage of the service which could lead to a high financial impact over the company.

Open the administrative tool named *server manager*, in order to install the required Link aggregation feature.

After opening the Server Manager, select the *Local Server* menu available on the left part of the screen and click on the *NIC teaming* option.

On the *NIC teaming windows*, locate the *team* configuration on the bottom left of the screen, select the *Tasks* menu and click on the *New Team* option.

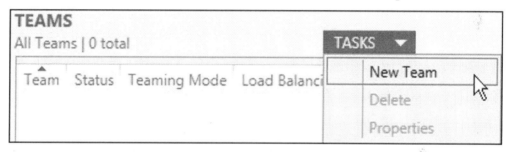

Enter an *identification name* for the virtual link aggregation interface, choose which physical interfaces should be members of this team, expand the *Additional properties* option, select the *lacp* teaming mode and the *Dynamic* load balancing mode.

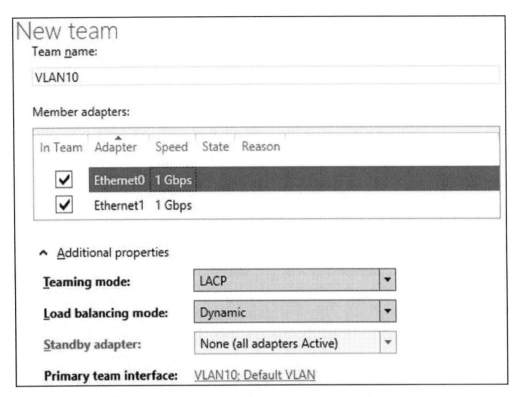

After finishing the team creation process, a new virtual network interface will be created on the Windows server using the identification name specified previously.

For safety reasons, the physical connection between the network switch and the file server should be performed only after both devices have been configured to use link aggregation.

Conclusion

This chapter taught using practical examples how to configure the link aggregation feature, in order to help the network administrator achieve better network performance and a level of redundancy.

Throughout this chapter, we were able to follow Luke while he configured a network switch to meet the following project requirements listed in the document called *requirements of the new network*.

- The connection between the network switches must be redundant
- The connection between the switch and the file server must be redundant

At the end of this chapter, the reader should be able to configure the link aggregation feature on a switch, in order to improve the performance and add redundancy to his network.

To improve the learning curve, the following video were published on our youtube channel showing how to use the techniques presented in this chapter:

• HP Switch – Configure link aggregation

– Chapter 09 –

CENTRALIZED AUTHENTICATION

In order to improve devices access management, Luke decided to integrate the switch's remote access authentication with the company's active directory domain through the use of a radius server.

The radius protocol uses a client-server architecture, in order to allow a radius server to authenticate remote users trying to access a client device, such as a network switch.

The use of radius allows a company to store user accounts and passwords in a central database, such as Microsoft Active Directory instead of storing that information locally on each of the switches.

This chapter will teach how to perform the configuration of a network switch to use radius authentication through a detailed step by step approach.

Throughout this chapter, the following tasks related to the implementation of the network project will be presented:

- How to setup a radius server
- How to configure radius authentication

All the lessons included in this chapter will be presented in a practical way using Luke's point of view during the implementation of his project.

Step by Step Guide

The radius authentication process is complex and requires full attention from the network administrator in order to understand and perform the many steps listed below.

As the first step, the network administrator needs to create two user groups that will offer different access levels to the network switches.

As the second step, the network administrator needs to perform the installation of a Radius server on a computer that will be responsible for the switch's remote access authentication.

As the third step, the network administrator needs to register all the network switches as client devices on the radius server and perform the configuration of the required authentication policies.

As the fourth and the final step, the network administrator needs to configure the network switches to redirect its remote user authentication to the radius server.

Creating a User Group

After a brief planning, it was decided that two groups of users should exist and offer different access levels to its members which are essentially IT analysts from the information technology staff.

In our example, members of the *fkit-admin* group should have all the administrative permissions available on the network switches while members of the *fkit-users* group should be able to access the device with read-only permissions.

In order to create the necessary user group, access the domain controller and open the administrative tool called *Active directory users and computers*.

On the active directory administration screen, do a right-click on the organizational unit called *Users*, select the menu *New* and click on the *Group* option.

Network Project with HP Switch

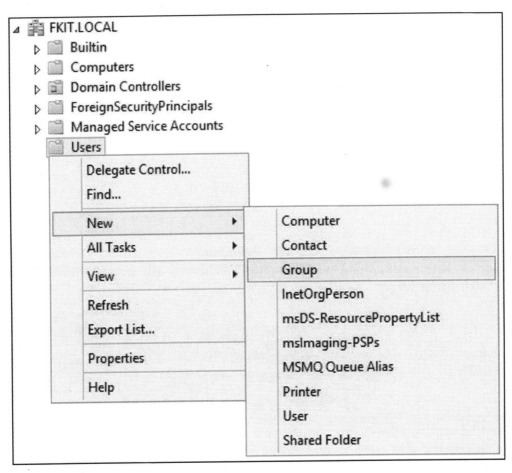

On the group creation screen, enter an identification name for the group with administrative permission over the switches and click on the *Ok* button.

CENTRALIZED AUTHENTICATION

Access the group properties, select the **Members** tab, add the users who should have administrative permission over the switches and click on the **Ok** button.

General	Members	Member Of	Managed By

Members:

Name	Active Directory Domain Services Folder
Luke S.	FKIT.LOCAL/Users

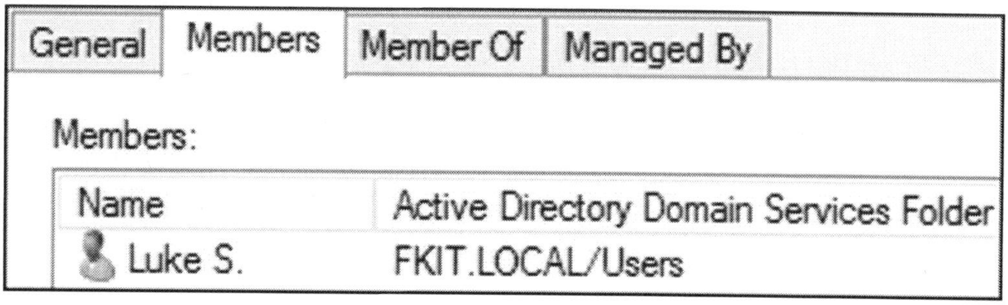

After finishing the administrative group configuration, create a new group that will receive read-only permission over the switches.

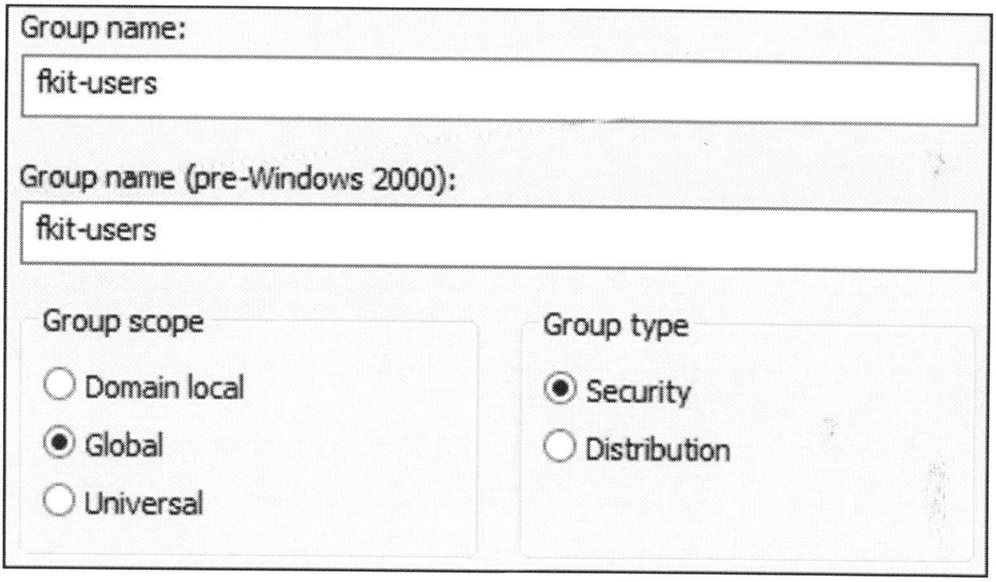

Group name:

fkit-users

Group name (pre-Windows 2000):

fkit-users

Group scope
- ○ Domain local
- ● Global
- ○ Universal

Group type
- ● Security
- ○ Distribution

Access the group properties, select the **Members** tab, add the users who should have a read-only permission over the switches and click on the **Ok** button.

General	Members	Member Of	Managed By

Members:

Name	Active Directory Domain Services Folder
Bill B	FKIT.LOCAL/Users
Leia S	FKIT.LOCAL/Users

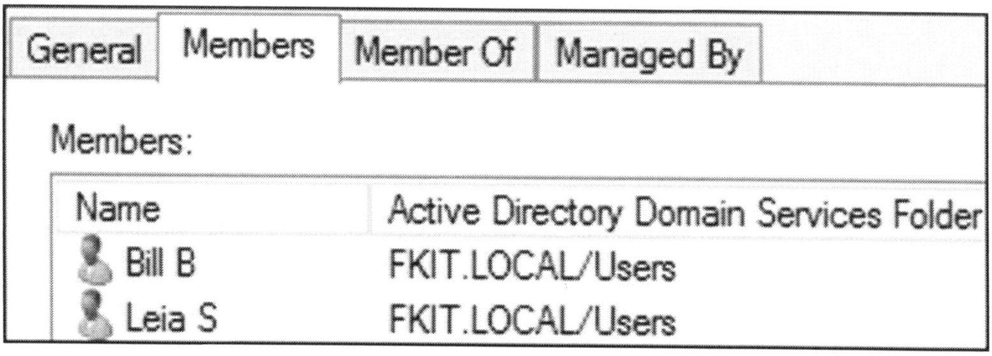

In our example, the network administrator created two groups. The first group, called *fkit-admins*, will receive the maximum administrative access level and the second group, called *fkit-users*, will receive a read-only access level.

Radius Server Installation

The radius server is the computer that will receive the username and password entered by the end user, in order to validate the authentication and set the proper authorization level.

In order to install a radius server, access a computer running Windows 2012 and open the administrative tool called *Server manager.*

On the server manager screen, open the *Manage* menu and select the *Add Roles and Features* option.

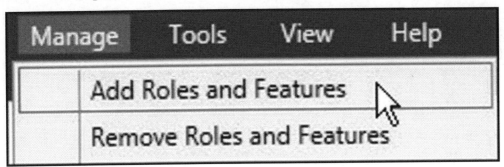

On the wizard screen, click on the *Next* button repeatedly until the *Select server roles screen* is displayed.

On the Select server roles screen, select the *Network Policy and Access Services* option, as shown.

CENTRALIZED AUTHENTICATION

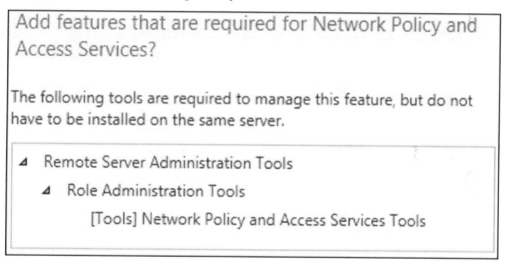

On the required features screen, click on the *Add features* button and then keep clicking on the *Next* button repeatedly until the installation is finished.

In our example, the network administrator installed the radius service on a computer running Windows 2012 standard.

Radius Server Configuration

After finishing the radius server installation, a couple of network access policies will need to be created, therefore, access the radius server using the domain administrator account and open the administrative tool called **Network Policy Server**.

91

On the network policy server screen, do a right-click on *NPS(LOCAL)* and select the ***Register server in Active Directory*** option, in order to authorize this computer to play the role of a Radius server.

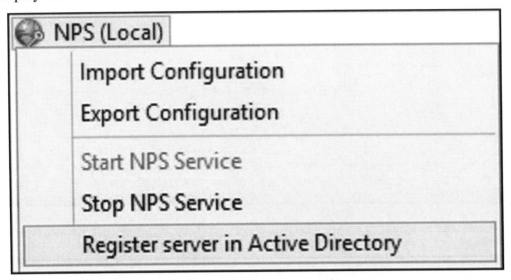

After confirming the decision to authorize the server to play the role of a radius server, this computer will be added as a member of the ***RAS and IAS Servers*** group.

As the next step, the network administrator needs to add the switches as clients on the radius server, therefore, expand the ***Radius clients and servers*** folder, do a right-click on ***Radius Clients*** and select the *New* option.

CENTRALIZED AUTHENTICATION

During the setup of a new radius client, the network administrator will need to set a *client identification name*, the client *IP address* and a *shared secret* used to authenticate the communication between the radius server and the client switch.

In our example, the network administrator created a new radius client named *fkit-sw01*, using the *192.168.1.11* address and the shared secret *kamisama123@*.

As the next step, the network administrator needs to create an access policy to the network switches, therefore, expand the *Policies* folder, do a right-click on *network policies* and select the *New* option.

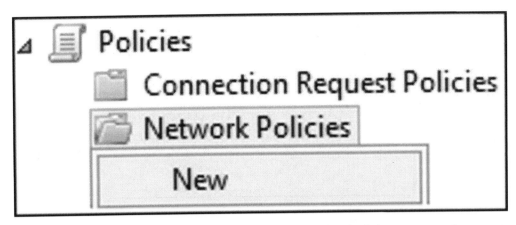

During the setup of a network policy, the network administrator needs to set a policy name, the access conditions and extra parameters unique to this brand of switches.

On the initial screen, enter a policy identification name and click on the *Next* button.

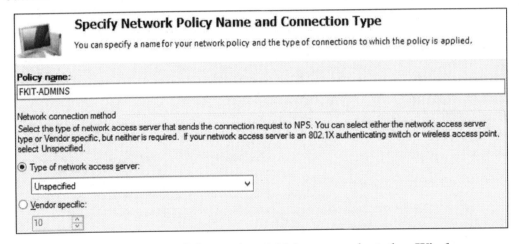

On the condition screen, click on the *Add* button, select the *Windows group* option and add an active directory group that should have administrative permission over the network switches.

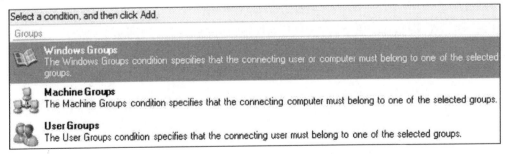

After finishing the configuration, be sure to check the summary of conditions before clicking on the *Next* button.

```
Specify the group membership required to match this policy.
Groups
FKIT\fkit-admin
```

On the next screen, the network administrator should select the *Access granted* option, in order to authorize the access to the switches to any user that comply the conditions set in this policy.

```
(•) Access granted
    Grant access if client connection attempts match the conditions of this policy.

( ) Access denied
    Deny access if client connection attempts match the conditions of this policy.

[ ] Access is determined by User Dial-in properties (which override NPS policy)
    Grant or deny access according to user dial-in properties if client connection attempts match the conditions of this policy.
```

In our example, the network administrator decided to grant access to a user that prove to be a member of the active directory group named *fkit-admin*.

On the next screen, the network administrator should configure a list of acceptable authentication protocols in the communication between the radius server and the client devices, therefore, select the *PAP* option and click on the *Next* button.

```
EAP types are negotiated between NPS and the client in the order in which they are listed.
EAP Types:

                                                     [ Move Up   ]
                                                     [ Move Down ]

[ Add... ]  [ Edit... ]  [ Remove ]

Less secure authentication methods:
[✓] Microsoft Encrypted Authentication version 2 (MS-CHAP-v2)
    [✓] User can change password after it has expired
[✓] Microsoft Encrypted Authentication (MS-CHAP)
    [✓] User can change password after it has expired
[ ] Encrypted authentication (CHAP)
[✓] Unencrypted authentication (PAP, SPAP)
[ ] Allow clients to connect without negotiating an authentication method.
[ ] Perform machine health check only
```

Network Project with HP Switch

If the following screen appears offering access to the help file, click on the *No* button and proceed to the next step.

> You selected one or more insecure authentication methods. To ensure that each protocol is correctly configured for the remote access, policy, and domain levels, follow the step-by-step procedures in Help.
>
> View the corresponding Help topic?

On the constraints setup screen, just click on the *Next* button and proceed to the next step.

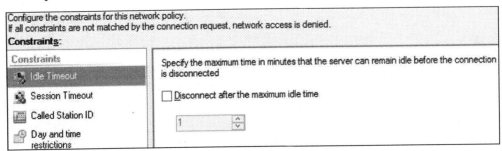

On the settings configuration screen, select and remove the standard radius attributes called *Framed-Protocol* and *Service-Type*.

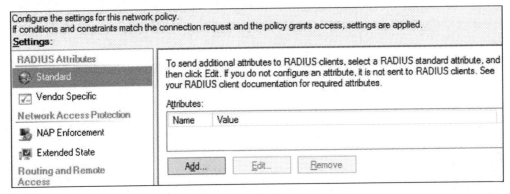

After removing both attributes, click on the *Add* button, choose the option *All* on the first combo box, select the *Service-Type* attribute and click on the *Add* button.

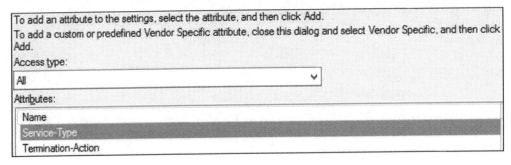

CENTRALIZED AUTHENTICATION

On the attribute information screen, select the *Others* option box, choose the *Login* attribute and click on the *OK* button.

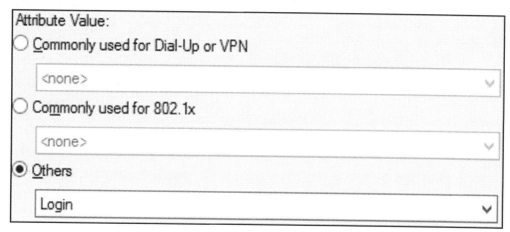

After finishing the configuration, be sure to check if the Service-Type radius attribute is displayed on the screen.

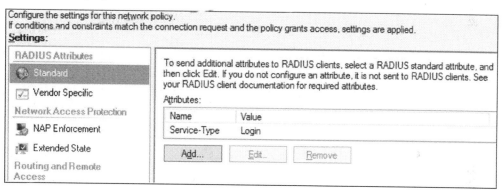

As a next step, select the *Vendor specific* radius attributes, click on the *Add* button, choose *All* on the Vendor combo box, select the *Vendor-specific* attribute and click on the *Add* button.

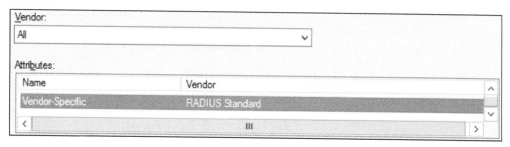

On the attribute information screen, click on the *Add* button.

97

Network Project with HP Switch

On the Vendor-specific attribute information screen, select the **Enter vendor code** option, enter the **25506** code to identify the HP vendor, select the **Yes** option and click on the **Configure Attribute** button.

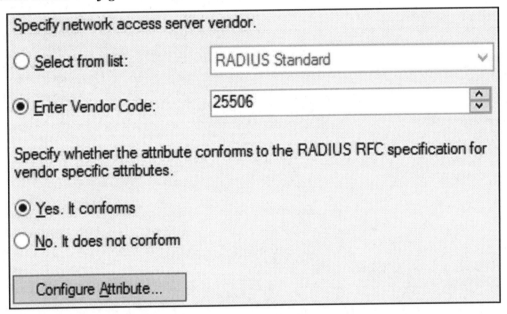

On the Configure VSA screen, enter the attribute **29** which identifies the user privilege level, select the **Decimal** attribute format, set the value as **3** which determines the maximum allowed administrative level and click on the **Ok** button.

CENTRALIZED AUTHENTICATION

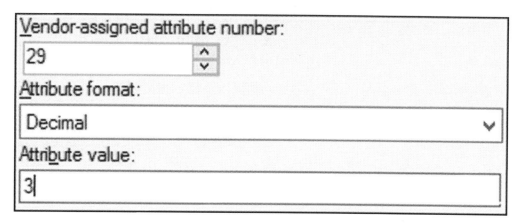

After finishing the configuration, be sure to check if the Vendor-Specific radius attribute is displayed on the screen before clicking on the *Next* button.

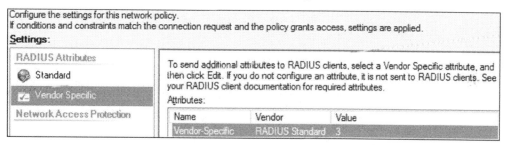

On the Summary screen, check the properties of the network policy and click on the ***Finish*** button, in order to complete the setup and activate the policy.

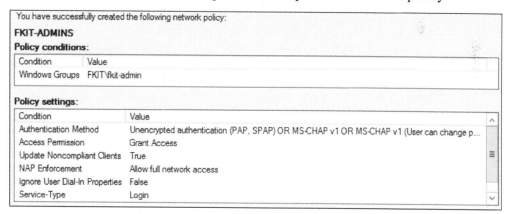

After finishing the privileged access policy setup, the network administrator needs to create the read-only access policy, therefore, let's duplicate the first policy created.

To duplicate an existing policy, Do a right-click on the previously created network policy and select the ***Duplicate Policy*** option.

After finishing the duplication process, a new policy will be generated using the same properties of the original policy, therefore, edit the duplicate policy by doing a right-click and selecting the *Properties* option.

On the policy edition screen, change the policy identification name, access the *Conditions tab* and change the active directory group to one containing users that should have read-only privileges over the switches.

As a next step, access the *Settings* tab, select the *Vendor-specific* radius attributes, and change the value 3 of the attribute *number 29 to 1*, in order to specify a read-only privilege to users authenticated by this network policy and finish the policy configuration process.

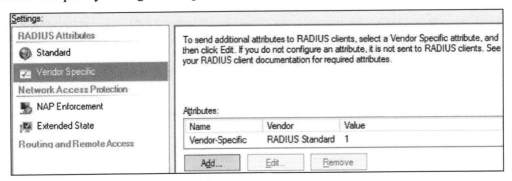

After finishing the duplication process, the network administrator needs to enable the new policy, therefore, do a right-click on the new policy and select the *Enable* option.

Keep in mind that the radius server policy processing is done in ascending order, therefore, the policies created for users with administrative or read-only privileges should be listed in the first and second position, as shown below.

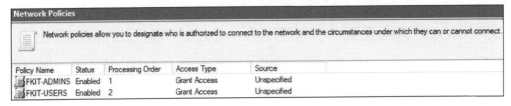

In our example, members of the group *fkit-admin* will have all the administrative permissions available on the network switches while members of the group *fkit-users* will be able to access the device with read-only permissions.

CENTRALIZED AUTHENTICATION

Setting Radius Authentication

After finishing the radius server configuration, the network administrator needs to configure the switches to use the radius server for user authentication.

Open the web interface, select the Authentication menu and click on the *Radius* option to be sent to the link aggregation management page.

In order to add a radius server, access the *Radius Server* tab, select the *Authentication Server* type, enter the radius server *IP address*, select the *Active* status and click on the *Apply* button.

Keep in mind that it is possible to add a second radius server that would be used, if the first server did not answer the request.

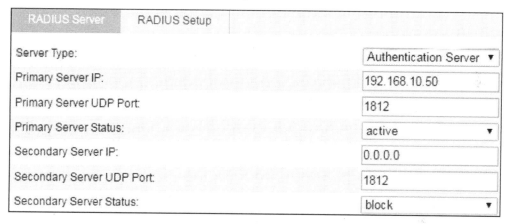

After adding the radius server to the switch, the network administrator should setup the communication settings, therefore, access the *Radius Setup* tab, select the *extended* server type, choose the *Authentication server shared key* check box, enter the *shared secret* previously configured on the radius server, change the username format to *Without-domain*, enter the *IP address* of the radius server in the Security policy server field and click on the *Apply* button.

Network Project with HP Switch

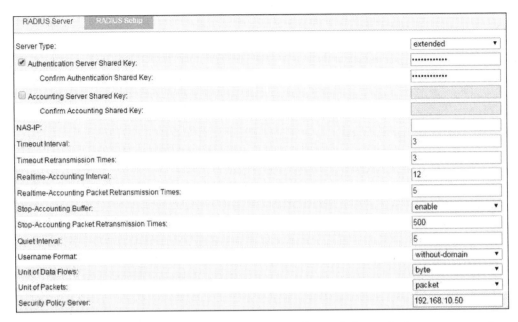

In our example, the network administrator configured the switch to communicate with the radius server 192.168.10.50, using an extended version of the radius protocol and the shared secret kamisama123@.

After finishing the communication setup, the network administrator needs to change the authentication domain of the switch to use the radius server, therefore, select the *Authentication* menu and click on the *AAA* option.

First, access the *Domain Setup* tab, add a new domain name to identify radius authenticated users, select the *Enable* option to setup this domain as the default authentication scheme and click on the *Apply* button.

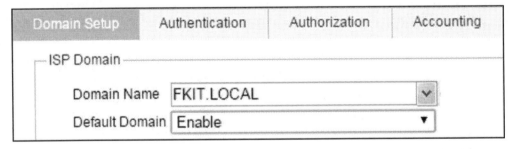

After finishing the domain configuration, access the *Authentication* tab, select the *domain* previously created, select the *Login AuthN* check box, select the *Radius* option, select the *System* name, set the secondary authentication method as *Local* and click on the *Apply* button.

CENTRALIZED AUTHENTICATION

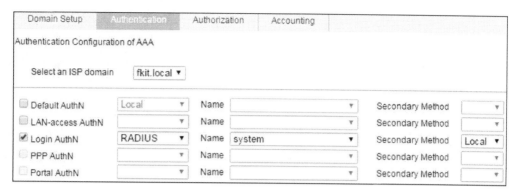

In our example, the network administrator created the fkit.local domain, configured the switch's authentication scheme to use the radius server to handle user authentications and set the local authentication to be used as a backup, in case the radius server is not answering the requests.

After finishing the authentication scheme configuration, access the *Authorization* tab, configure the *Login AuthZ* checkbox the same way it was done before and click on the *Apply* button.

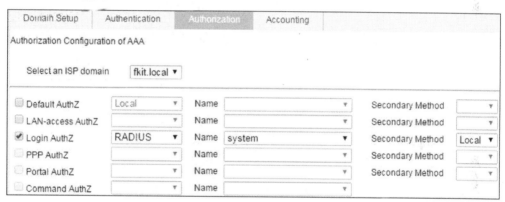

In order to test your configuration, click on the *Logout* option available at the top right of the screen, try to log in again to the web interface using an active directory account that is a member of the administrative or read-only group and make sure the menus are being displayed in according to the access level configured.

After finishing the radius authentication configuration, be sure to save your settings by clicking on the *Save* option available at the top right of the screen.

It is possible that some readers prefer to use the command-line instead of the web interface, therefore, we will also teach you how to configure the radius authentication using the command-line.

Using either the console, telnet or ssh, connect to the command-line of your switch and log in with a user who has administrative privileges.

Network Project with HP Switch

If available to your switch model, enter the **_cmdline-mode** command in order to access the secret command-line mode of the device.

```
# _cmdline-mode on
```

Use the **system-view** command to enter the configuration mode.

```
# system-view
```

Create a radius authentication scheme called System, enable the extended version of the radius protocol, register the IP address of the radius server and enter the shared secret previously configured on the radius server.

```
# radius scheme system
# server-type extended
# primary authentication 192.168.10.50
# security-policy-server 192.168.10.50
# key authentication simple kamisama123@
# user-name-format without-domain
```

Use the following command to check your configuration.

```
# display radius scheme
```

Create a new authentication domain, configure the switch's authentication and authorization to use radius as the primary method to handle user authentications and set the local authentication to be used as a backup method, in case the radius server is not answering the requests.

```
# domain fkit.local
# authentication login radius-scheme system local
# authorization login radius-scheme system local
```

After finishing the configuration set this domain as the default authentication domain.

```
# domain default enable fkit.local
```

Use the following command to check your configuration.

```
# display domain fkit.local
```

Save your settings by using the command below.

```
# save
```

If you need to remove the radius authentication, enter the configuration mode and use the following command.

```
# undo domain fkit.local
# undo radius scheme system
```

Conclusion

This chapter taught using practical examples how to configure the radius authentication feature, in order to help the network administrator achieve centralized authentication.

Throughout this chapter, we were able to follow Luke while he configured a network switch to meet the following project requirements listed in the document called ***requirements of the new network***.

- It must be possible to integrate the authentication with active directory
- It must be possible to use different access levels to the switches

At the end of this chapter, the reader should be able to configure radius authentication on a switch, in order to improve the control of his network through centralized authentication.

To improve the learning curve, the following videos were published on our youtube channel showing how to use the techniques presented in this chapter:

- IIP Switch – Radius Authentication
- Windows 2012 – Radius Server Installation

– Chapter 10 –

NETWORK MONITORING

After finishing the installation and configuration of the devices, Luke decides it's time to add the switches to the existing network monitoring system managed by the linux specialists.

A network monitoring system may be described as one or more applications that enable the remote collection of information about the configuration and performance of network devices.

Through the use of snmp, the network administrator is able to authorize the network monitoring system to collect information remotely from a switch.

The snmp protocol was designed to standardize the remote collection of data between two devices through the use of a basic question and answer system.

This chapter will teach how to enable and configure snmp on a network switch through a detailed step by step approach.

Throughout this chapter, the following tasks related to the implementation of the network project will be presented:

- How to configure SNMP version 2c
- How to configure SNMP version 3

All the lessons included in this chapter will be presented in a practical way using Luke's point of view during the implementation of his project.

SNMP Configuration

After a meeting with the stakeholders, it was decided that all switches of the network project should be added to the existing network monitoring system, which is currently managed by the Linux specialist team.

In our example, the network switches should have the snmp service enabled and configured, in order for the network monitoring system be able to collect information remotely.

Open the web interface, access the **Device** menu and click on the **SNMP** option to be sent to the snmp service management page.

NETWORK MONITORING

In order to enable snmp, access the **Setup** tab, select the **Enable** option, set a contact person, the equipment location, choose the *v2c* version and click the *Apply* button.

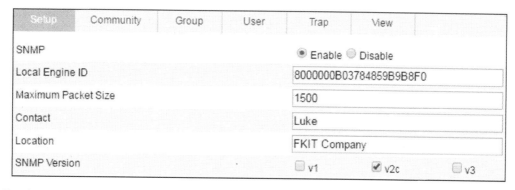

During setup of the snmp service, the network administrator will need to choose which version of the snmp protocol should be enabled, therefore, here we present a list of versions available and their descriptions.

The *snmp version 1* provides only a basic request and response system between two devices that prove the knowledge of a shared secret, known as snmp community.

The *snmp version 2c* added improvements and new features related to the exchange of information between devices.

The *snmp version 3* introduced an information security layer capable of offer features such as user authentication and encryption.

After a meeting with the linux specialists team, Luke decided to use the snmp protocol version 2c instead of the version 3, because the current network monitoring system does not support snmp version 3.

After enabling the service, the network administrator will have to create a snmp community in order to authorize the communication between the network monitoring system and the switch, therefore, access the **Community** tab, click on the *Add* button, enter a community name, select the *read-only* access right and click on the *Apply* button.

Network Project with HP Switch

After finishing the snmp service configuration, the network administrator needs to test the snmp communication, therefore visit the *paessler.com* website and download the *Paessler SNMP Tester software*.

To test the SNMP communication, open the *Paessler SNMP Tester software*, type the IP address of the switch, select *the 2c protocol version*, enter the *snmp community*, select the *Read device uptime* option and click on the *Start* button.

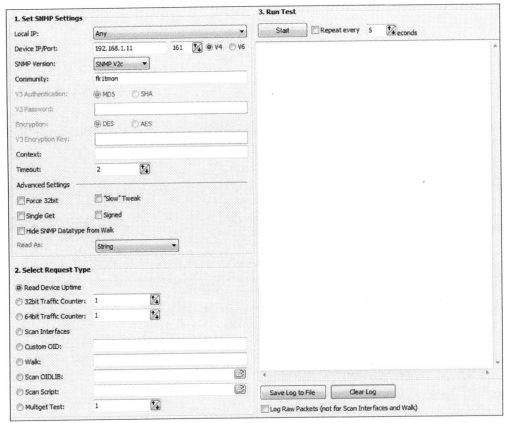

In our example, the snmp service version 2c was enabled and a snmp community called *fk1tmon* was created with read-only permissions

After finishing the snmp service setup, be sure to save your settings by clicking on the *Save* option available at the top right of the screen.

It is possible that some readers prefer to use the command-line instead of the web interface, therefore, we will also teach you how to setup the snmp service using the command-line.

Using either the console, telnet or ssh, connect to the command-line of your switch and log in with a user who has administrative privileges.

If available to your switch model, enter the *_cmdline-mode* command in order to access the secret command-line mode of the device.

NETWORK MONITORING

```
# cmdline-mode on
```

Use the ***system-view*** command to enter the configuration mode.

```
# system-view
```

Use the following commands to enable snmp version 2c, set a contact person and the device location.

```
# snmp-agent
# snmp-agent sys-info version v2c
# snmp-agent sys-info contact Luke
# snmp-agent sys-info location FKIT Company
```

Create a snmp community with read-only permission.

```
# snmp-agent community read fk1tm0n
```

Use the following command to check your configuration.

```
# display snmp-agent sys-info
# display snmp-agent community
```

Save your settings by using the command below.

```
# save
```

To delete a snmp community, enter the configuration mode and use the following command.

```
# undo snmp-agent community read fk1tm0n
```

Use the following command to disable the snmp service on the switch.

```
# undo snmp-agent
# undo snmp-agent sys-info version v2c
```

SNMPv3 Configuration

After assessing the network monitoring solution used by the Linux Specialists team, Luke came to the conclusion that it does not support the snmp version 3, therefore, the following configuration will be demonstrated for educational purposes only.

Open the web interface, access the ***Device*** menu and click on the ***SNMP*** option to be sent to the snmp service management page.

In order to enable snmp, access the ***Setup*** tab, select the ***Enable*** option, keep the default local engine identification, set a contact person, the location of equipment, select the ***v3*** version and click on the ***Apply*** button.

Network Project with HP Switch

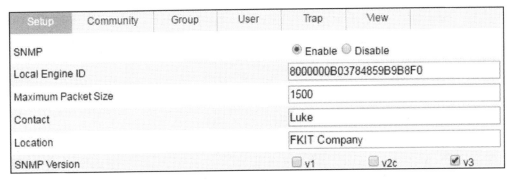

After enabling snmp, the network administrator should create a group of permissions, therefore, access the **Group** tab, click on the **Add** button, enter a group name, select the **AuthPriv** security level, set the **Read view** option as **Viewdefault** and click on the **Apply** button.

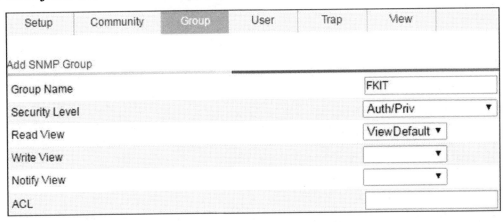

In our example, the snmp service version 3 was enabled and the highest security level, AuthPriv, was configured with read-only permissions.

In order to create a new snmp user, access the **User** tab, click on the **Add** button, enter a username, select **AuthPriv** security level, select the group created previously, select the **SHA** authentication mode, enter a user authentication password, select the **AES128** privacy mode, enter a communication encryption password and click on the **Add** button.

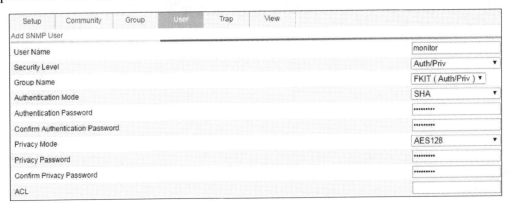

NETWORK MONITORING

During the setup of a new snmp user, the network administrator will need to choose which security level should be used, therefore, here we present a list of the available options and their descriptions.

The *noAuthNoPriv* level provides no authentication and no encryption to the snmp communication.

The *AuthNoPriv* level provides authentication through a username and password combination but does not offer encryption to the snmp communication.

The *AuthPriv* level provides authentication through a username and password combination together with the encryption of the snmp communication through the use of a shared secret.

In our example, we configured a snmp user named *monitor* with the *AuthPriv* security level, the *SHA* authentication algorithm was used with the *123456789* password while the *AES128* encryption algorithm was used with the *987654321* shared secret.

After finishing the snmp service configuration, the network administrator needs to test the snmp communication, therefore visit the *paessler.com* website and download the *Paessler SNMP Tester software*.

To test the SNMP communication, open the *Paessler SNMP Tester software*, type the IP *address of the network switch*, select the protocol *version 3*, select the *SHA* algorithm, select the *AES* algorithm, enter the snmp *username* previously created, enter the *authentication password*, enter the *shared secret* for encryption, select the *Read device uptime* option and click on the *Start* button.

Network Project with HP Switch

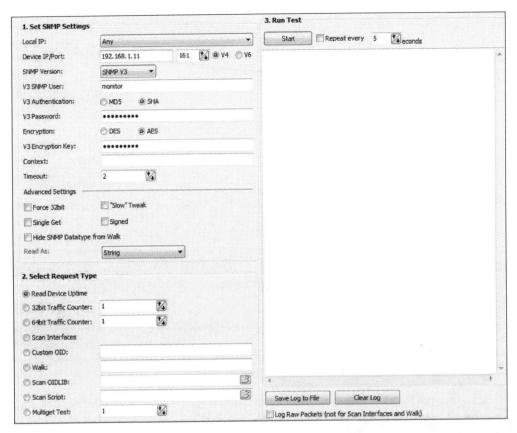

In our example, the snmp service version 3 was enabled, a user named monitor with the *AuthPriv* security level was created using the *SHA* authentication algorithm and the *123456789* password while the *AES128* encryption algorithm was used with the *987654321* shared secret.

After finishing the snmp service setup, be sure to save your settings by clicking on the *Save* option available at the top right of the screen.

It is possible that some readers prefer to use the command-line instead of the web interface, therefore, we will also teach you how to setup the snmp service using the command-line.

Using either the console, telnet or ssh, connect to the command-line of your switch and log in with a user who has administrative privileges.

If available to your switch model, enter the *_cmdline-mode* command in order to access the secret command-line mode of the device.

_cmdline-mode on

Use the *system-view* command to enter the configuration mode.

system-view

NETWORK MONITORING

Use the following commands to enable snmp version 3, set a contact person and the device location.

```
# snmp-agent
# snmp-agent sys-info version v3
# snmp-agent sys-info contact Luke
# snmp-agent sys-info location FKIT Company
```

Create a snmp group with the security level Authpriv.

```
# snmp-agent group v3 FKIT privacy
```

Create a snmp user with authentication and encryption passwords.

```
# snmp-agent usm-user v3 monitor FKIT authentication-mode sha 123456789 privacy-mode aes128 987654321
```

In our example, we configured a snmp user named *monitor* with the security level *Authpriv*, the *sha* authentication algorithm and the authentication password *123456789*, the *aes128* encryption algorithm and encryption password *987654321*.

Use the following command to check your configuration.

```
# display snmp-agent sys-info
# display snmp-agent usm-user
```

Save your settings by using the command below.

```
# save
```

To delete a snmp user, enter the configuration mode and use the following command.

```
# undo snmp-agent usm-user v3 monitor FKIT local
```

Use the following command to disable the snmp service on the switch.

```
# undo snmp-agent
# undo snmp-agent sys-info version v3
```

Conclusion

This chapter taught using practical examples how to enable and configure the snmp feature, in order to help the network administrator achieve better network performance monitoring.

Throughout this chapter, we were able to follow Luke while he configured a network switch to meet the following project requirements listed in the document called ***requirements of the new network***.

• It must be possible to monitor the network switches via snmp

At the end of this chapter, the reader should be able to configure the snmp service on a switch, in order to monitor his switch using a network monitoring application.

To improve the learning curve, the following video were published on our youtube channel showing how to use the techniques presented in this chapter:

• HP Switch – SNMP Configuration
• HP Switch – SNMPv3 Configuration

– Chapter 11 –

PORT MONITORING

After finishing the snmp configuration and add the switches to the existing network monitoring system, Luke noticed that a switch port was improperly using a high data transfer rate and decides to investigate the incident.

The use of techniques such as port mirroring offers a quick way for the network administrators to analyze a network issue, in order to find the root cause of a problem.

Port mirroring is a technique that can be used to monitor the network traffic of a switch port by replicating all input and output packets to a destination port which will perform the role of monitor interface.

This chapter will teach how to configure port mirroring on a network switch through a detailed step by step approach.

Throughout this chapter, the following tasks related to the implementation of the network project will be presented:

• How to configure port mirroring

All the lessons included in this chapter will be presented in a practical way using Luke's point of view during the implementation of his project.

Port Mirroring

Upon receiving a network monitoring system alert message about high network throughput over port 20, Luke decided to investigate what is going on by using the port mirroring technique to replicate all the packets sent and received by port 20 to port 10.

In our example, all packets sent and received by port 20 should be replicated to the port 10 which will be connected to a computer running a network traffic analyzer software.

The port mirroring configuration will enable a computer connected to port 10 to monitor all the network traffic of the suspect computer which is connected to port 20.

Open the web interface, access the *Device* menu and click on the *Port Mirroring* option to be sent to the port mirroring management page.

In order to enable port mirroring, select the *Create* tab, enter a numeric identifier to the monitoring group, choose the *local* type and click on the *Apply* button.

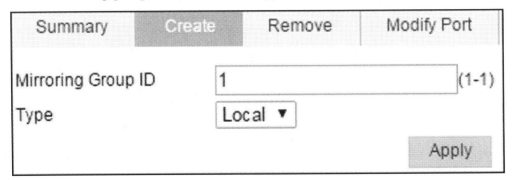

To configure the port responsible for monitoring, select the *Modify port* tab, choose the monitoring group identification created before, set the port type as *monitor*, select the switch port that will be responsible for monitoring and click the *Apply* button.

To configure the port that will be monitored, select the *Modify port* tab, choose the monitoring group identification created before, set the port type as *mirror*, select the switch port that needs to be monitored and click on the *Apply* button.

In order to verify your configuration, select the *Summary* tab and check the summary of your mirroring configuration.

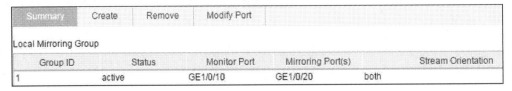

From this moment on, all input and output packets from the switch port 20 will automatically be replicated to the port 10 of the same switch, therefore, as the last step, the network administrator should download and install a software able to analyze the network traffic on the computer connected to the switch port 10.

After finishing the port mirroring configuration, the network administrator needs a software to monitor the suspect computer communication, therefore visit the *wireshark.org* website and download **Wireshark** software.

After performing the Wireshark installation properly with **Winpcap support enabled**, the network administrator will be able to view the replicated network traffic through its graphical user interface as shown below.

No.	Time	Source	Destination	Protocol
1	0.000000	192.168.20.50	108.179.252.167	TCP
18	0.250470	192.168.20.50	108.179.252.167	TCP
1155	29.409489	192.168.20.50	108.179.252.167	TCP
1156	29.409871	192.168.20.50	108.179.252.167	TCP
1172	29.660197	192.168.20.50	108.179.252.167	TCP

In our example, the input and output traffic from the switch port 20 were replicated to port 10, which is connected to a computer running a network analysis software.

After analyzing the captured traffic, the network administrator found that the device connected to the switch port 20 is Leia's workstation, which is consuming a large piece of the company's Internet bandwidth to do downloads from the website www.fucking-it.com which uses the IP address 108.179.252.167.

It is important to highlight that a low point of this technique is the excessive consumption of the switch's processor and memory due to the traffic replication to the monitoring port, therefore, a network administrator should use the mirroring technique only for a short period and remove it as soon as the problem identified has been resolved.

It is possible that some readers prefer to use the command-line instead of the web interface, therefore, we will also teach you how to setup a port mirroring using the command-line.

Using either the console, telnet or ssh, connect to the command-line of your switch and log in with a user who has administrative privileges.

Network Project with HP Switch

If available to your switch model, enter the *_cmdline-mode* command in order to access the secret command-line mode of the device.

```
# _cmdline-mode on
```

Use the *system-view* command to enter the configuration mode.

```
# system-view
```

Create a monitoring group using the following command.

```
# mirroring-group 1 local
```

After the creation of the monitoring group, associate the switch port 10 to this group using the monitoring mode.

```
# interface GigabitEthernet1/0/10
# mirroring-group 1 monitor-port
```

Associate the switch port 20 to this group using the mirroring mode.

```
# interface GigabitEthernet1/0/20
# mirroring-group 1 mirroring-port both
```

Use the following command to check your configuration.

```
# display mirroring-group 1
```

Save your settings by using the command below.

```
# save
```

To disable port mirroring, enter the configuration mode and use the following command.

```
# undo mirroring-group 1
```

Conclusion

This chapter taught using practical examples how to configure the port mirroring feature, in order to help the network administrator find the root cause of a network issue.

Throughout this chapter, we were able to follow Luke while he configured a network switch to meet the following project requirements listed in the document called ***requirements of the new network***.

• It must be possible to monitor the traffic of an interface through mirroring

At the end of this chapter, the reader should be able to configure port mirroring on a network switch, in order to help diagnose a network issue.

To improve the learning curve, the following video were published on our youtube channel showing how to use the techniques presented in this chapter:

• HP Switch – Configure port mirroring
• Windows – Wireshark Installation

– Chapter 12 –

PACKET FILTER

Upon receiving a warning message from the network monitoring system about a high network throughput over port 20, Luke used the port mirroring technique to investigate and discovered that the computer connected to port 20 was doing countless downloads from the website www.fucking-it.com.

After analyzing the traffic, Luke decided to use the packet filter technique in order to block any access to the www.fucking-it.com website.

The use of a packet filter technique provides a quick and easy way for a network administrator to deny access to specific IP addresses and therefore, increase his control over a network.

This chapter will teach you how to configure packet filtering on a network switch through a detailed step by step approach.

Throughout this chapter, the following tasks related to the implementation of the network project will be presented:

• How to filter access to specific IP addresses

All the lessons included in this chapter will be presented in a practical way using Luke's point of view during the implementation of his project.

Step by Step Guide

The packet filtering process is complex and requires full attention from the network administrator in order to understand and perform the many steps required.

As the first step, the network administrator needs to create an access-list containing all the IP addresses that should be blocked.

As the second step, the network administrator needs to create a traffic class that will be used to classify the network traffic as a member of the IP address blacklist or not.

As the third step, the network administrator needs to create a behavior that will be used in response to any traffic classified as a member of the blacklist.

As a fourth step, the network administrator needs to create a traffic policy that will bring together all the items created before.

PACKET FILTER

In our example, the policy created will use the classification rule to detect any member of the access-list and use the behavior defined, in order to decide if the network packet should be allowed or denied

As the fifth and final step, the network administrator needs to apply the created policy on a switch port.

Access List Creation

As the first step, the network administrator needs to create an access-list containing the IP addresses that should be blocked.

Open the web interface, select the **QoS** menu and click on the **ACL IPV4** option to be sent to the access-list management page.

In order to create a new access-list, select the **Create** tab, enter a numeric identifier to the new access-list and click on the **Apply** button.

Summary	Create	Basic Setup	Advanced Setup	Link Layer Setup	Remove
ACL Number	3000		2000-2999 for basic ACLs. 3000-3999 for advanced ACLs. 4000-4999 for Ethernet frame header ACLs.		
Match Order	Config ▼				

During the setup of a new access-list, the network administrator will need to set a numeric identifier which represents the type of list being created, therefore, here we present the available options and their descriptions.

A numeric identifier *between 2000 and 2999* specifies the basic type of access-list which allows only the configuration of source addresses.

A numeric identifier *between 3000 and 2999* specifies the advanced type of access-list which allows the configuration of source and destination IP addresses along with the protocol type, source, and destination port.

A numeric identifier *between 4000 and 4999* specifies a layer 2 which allows the configuration of MAC addresses and other layer 2 protocol information.

After finishing the creation of an advanced access-list, access the *Advanced Setup* tab, choose the access-list created before, select the *Deny* action, select the *destination address* check box and type the IP address which should be blocked.

Network Project with HP Switch

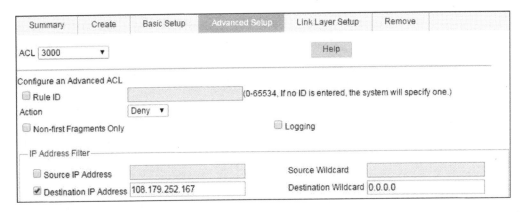

Also in the *Advanced Security* tab, select the protocol type you want to block and click on the *Add* button.

In our example, the network administrator created and configured the advanced access-list 3000 to block any traffic to the IP address 108.179.252.167 which is the IP address of the website www.fucking-it.com.

To check your settings, access the *Summary* tab and verify if the information displayed is correct.

After finishing the creation of an advanced access-list, be sure to save your settings by clicking on the *Save* option available at the top right of the screen.

If you need to remove an access-list, access the *Remove* tab, select the access-list desired and click on the *Remove* button.

It is possible that some readers prefer to use the command-line instead of the web interface, therefore, we will also teach you how to create an access-list using the command-line.

Using either the console, telnet or ssh, connect to the command-line of your switch and log in with a user who has administrative privileges.

If available to your switch model, enter the *_cmdline-mode* command in order to access the secret command-line mode of the device.

```
# cmdline-mode on
```

Use the *system-view* command to enter the configuration mode.

```
# system-view
```

PACKET FILTER

Create a new advanced access list, add a description and set the desired rules.

```
# acl number 3000
# description BLACKLIST-IP
# rule 0 deny ip destination 108.179.252.167 0.0.0.0
```

Use the following command to check your configuration.

```
# display acl 3000
```

Save your settings by using the command below.

```
# save
```

To remove an access-list, enter the configuration mode and use the following command.

```
# undo acl number 3000
```

Access Class Creation

As the second step, the network administrator needs to create a traffic class that will be used to classify the network traffic as a member of the IP address blacklist.

Open the web interface, select the *QoS* menu and click on the *Classifier* option to be sent to the traffic class setup page.

In order to create a new access class, select the *Create* tab, enter an identification name to the new class and click on the *Apply* button.

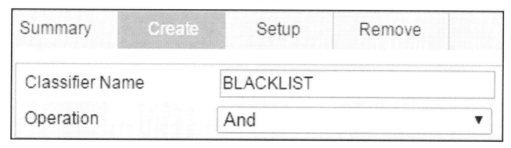

After finishing the creation of a traffic class, access the *Setup* tab, choose the class previously created, select the *ACL IPV4* box, type the previously created access-list number and click on the *Apply* button.

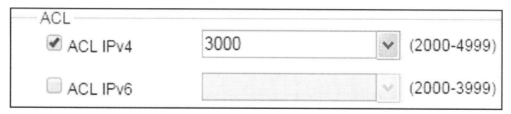

123

In our example, the network administrator created a traffic class named blacklist and configured the access-list 3000 as a way to identify if an IP address is a member of this class.

To check your settings, access the *Summary* tab and verify if the information displayed is correct.

After finishing the creation of a traffic class, be sure to save your settings by clicking on the *Save* option available at the top right of the screen.

If you need to remove a traffic class, access the *Remove* tab, select the access-list desired and click on the *Remove* button.

It is possible that some readers prefer to use the command-line instead of the web interface, therefore, we will also teach you how to create a traffic class using the command-line.

Using either the console, telnet or ssh, connect to the command-line of your switch and log in with a user who has administrative privileges.

If available to your switch model, enter the *_cmdline-mode* command in order to access the secret command-line mode of the device.

```
# _cmdline-mode on
```

Use the *system-view* command to enter the configuration mode.

```
# system-view
```

Create a new traffic class and assign the access-list previously created.

```
# traffic classifier BLACKLIST operator and
# if-match acl 3000
```

Use the following command to check your configuration.

```
# display traffic classifier user-defined BLACKLIST
```

Save your settings by using the command below.

```
# save
```

To remove a traffic class, enter the configuration mode and use the following command.

```
# undo traffic classifier BLACKLIST
```

Behavior Creation

As the third step, the network administrator needs to create a behavior that will be used in response to any traffic classified as a member of the blacklist.

Open the web interface, select the **QoS** menu and click on the **Behavior** option to be sent to the behavior management page.

In order to create a new behavior, select the **Create** tab, enter an identification name to the new behavior and click on the **Create** button.

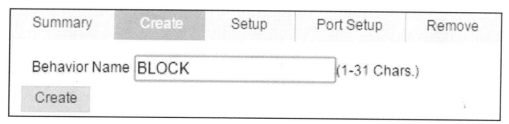

After finishing the behavior creation, access the **Setup** tab, choose the previously created behavior, select the *filter box*, select the **Deny** option and click on the **Apply** button.

In our example, the network administrator created a behavior identified as block that will eventually deny access to any IP address classified as a member of the blacklist class.

To check your settings, access the **Summary** tab and verify if the information displayed is correct.

After finishing the creation of behavior, be sure to save your settings by clicking on the **Save** option available at the top right of the screen.

If you need to remove a behavior, access the **Remove** tab, select the behavior desired and click on the **Remove** button.

It is possible that some readers prefer to use the command-line instead of the web interface, therefore, we will also teach you how to create a behavior using the command-line.

Using either the console, telnet or ssh, connect to the command-line of your switch and log in with a user who has administrative privileges.

If available to your switch model, enter the _*cmdline-mode*_ command in order to access the secret command-line mode of the device.

cmdline-mode on

Use the ***system-view*** command to enter the configuration mode.

system-view

Create a new behavior and configure it to deny access.

traffic behavior BLOCK
filter deny

Use the following command to check your configuration.

display traffic behavior user-defined BLOCK

Save your settings by using the command below.

save

To remove a behavior, enter the configuration mode and use the following command.

undo traffic behavior BLOCK

Create Access Policy

As the fourth step, the network administrator needs to create a traffic policy that will eventually be applied to the desired switch ports to enforce a behavior.

Open the web interface, select the ***QoS*** menu and click on the ***QoS Policy*** option to be sent to the traffic policy management page.

To create a new policy, select the ***Create*** option, enter an identification name to the new policy and click on the ***Create*** button.

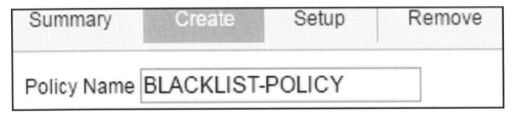

After finishing the creation of a policy, access the ***Setup*** tab, choose the desired ***traffic class***, select the desired ***behavior*** and click on the ***Apply*** button.

PACKET FILTER

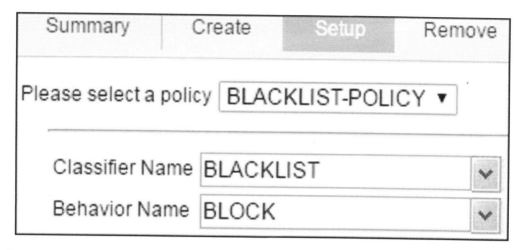

In our example, the network administrator created a traffic policy identified as blacklist-policy that will deny access to any network packet classified as a member of the blacklist class.

To check your settings, access the **Summary** tab and verify if the information displayed is correct.

After finishing the creation of policy, be sure to save your settings by clicking on the **Save** option available at the top right of the screen.

If you need to remove a policy, access the **Remove** tab, select the policy desired and click on the **Remove** button.

It is possible that some readers prefer to use the command-line instead of the web interface, therefore, we will also teach you how to create a traffic policy using the command-line.

Using either the console, telnet or ssh, connect to the command-line of your switch and log in with a user who has administrative privileges.

If available to your switch model, enter the **_cmdline-mode** command in order to access the secret command-line mode of the device.

```
# _cmdline-mode on
```

Use the **system-view** command to enter the configuration mode.

```
# system-view
```

Create a new access policy, add a traffic classification rule and the desired behavior.

```
# qos policy BLACKLIST-POLICY
# classifier BLACKLIST behavior BLOCK
```

Use the following command to check your configuration.

127

```
# display qos policy user-defined BLACKLIST-POLICY
```

Save your settings by using the command below.

```
# save
```

To delete a policy, enter the configuration mode and use the following command.

```
# undo qos policy BLACKLIST-POLICY
```

Applying the Access Policy

As the last step, the network administrator needs to apply the previously created traffic policy to a switch port, in order to enforce the desired behavior.

Open the web interface, select the *QoS* menu and click on the *Port Policy* option to be sent to the policy application page.

To apply a policy, access the *Setup* option, select the desired switch port, select the desired policy, select the *inbound* direction and click on the *Apply* button.

In our example, the network administrator applied the traffic policy identified as blacklist-policy to the switch port 20.

To check your settings, access the *Summary* tab and verify if the information displayed is correct.

After finishing the policy application, be sure to save your settings by clicking on the *Save* option available at the top right of the screen.

If you need to remove a policy applied, access the *Remove* tab, select the policy desired and click on the *Remove* button.

It is possible that some readers prefer to use the command-line instead of the web interface, therefore, we will also teach you how to apply a traffic policy using the command-line.

Using either the console, telnet or ssh, connect to the command-line of your switch and log in with a user who has administrative privileges.

If available to your switch model, enter the *_cmdline-mode* command in order to access the secret command-line mode of the device.

```
# cmdline-mode on
```

Use the ***system-view*** command to enter the configuration mode.

```
# system-view
```

Apply the traffic policy to the desired switch port.

```
# interface GigabitEthernet1/0/20
# qos apply policy BLACKLIST-POLICY inbound
```

Use the following command to check your configuration.

```
# display qos policy interface GigabitEthernet1/0/20
```

Save your settings by using the command below.

```
# save
```

To remove a policy application, enter the configuration mode and use the following command.

```
# interface GigabitEthernet1/0/20
# undo qos apply policy BLACKLIST-POLICY inbound
```

Conclusion

This chapter taught using practical examples how to configure the packet filter feature, in order to help the network administrator enforce a traffic policy and achieve better control over the network.

Throughout this chapter, we were able to follow Luke while he configured a network switch to meet the following project requirements listed in the document called ***requirements of the new network***.

• It must be possible to block access to specific IP addresses through rules

At the end of this chapter, the reader should be able to configure the packet filtering feature on a switch, in order to improve the security of his network.

To improve the learning curve, the following video were published on our youtube channel showing how to use the techniques presented in this chapter:

• HP Switch – Packet Filtering

– Chapter 13 –

BANDWIDTH LIMITATION

Upon receiving a warning message from the network monitoring system about the total utilization of the main internet link for several days, Luke used the port mirroring technique to investigate and discovered that the computer connected to port 12 was using a torrent software to do inappropriate downloads.

After analyzing the traffic, Luke decided to use a bandwidth limitation technique, in order to restrict the suspect computer to a maximum bandwidth of 50 Kilobytes.

The use of techniques such as traffic shaper provides a quick way for a network administrator enforce the maximum bandwidth available to a switch port and therefore, increase his control over a network.

This chapter will teach how to perform the configuration of traffic shaping through a detailed step by step approach.

Throughout this chapter, the following tasks related to the implementation of the network project will be presented:

• How to limit the bandwidth on an interface

All the lessons included in this chapter will be presented in a practical way using Luke's point of view during the implementation of his project.

Traffic Shaping

After detecting the root cause of the incident, Luke decided to limit the maximum bandwidth allowed on the switch port 12 as a short term solution.

Open the web interface, select the *QoS* menu and click on the *GTS* option to be sent to the generic traffic shaper configuration page.

In order to configure a bandwidth limitation, access the *Setup* tab, select the desired port, *enable* generic traffic shaper and enter the maximum speed in *kilobits*.

During the setup, the system requires the bandwidth information to be typed in *kilobits per second*, therefore, here we present a list of possible ways to calculate the desired bandwidth in kilobits.

BANDWIDTH LIMITATION

To convert from **Kilobytes** to **Kilobits**, the network administrator should multiply the value in kilobytes per 8. As an example, we can state that 50 kilobytes multiplied by 8 are equal to 400 kilobits.

To convert from **Megabytes** to **Kilobits**, the network administrator should multiply the value in megabytes per 8000. As an example, we can say that 2 megabytes multiplied by 8000 are equal to 16000 kilobits.

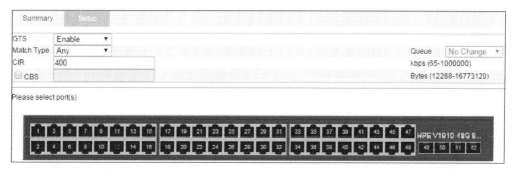

In our example, the network administrator restricted the switch port 12 to a maximum bandwidth of 50 Kilobytes, which are equivalent to 400 Kilobits.

To check your settings, access the **Summary** tab, select the desired network interface and verify if the information displayed is correct.

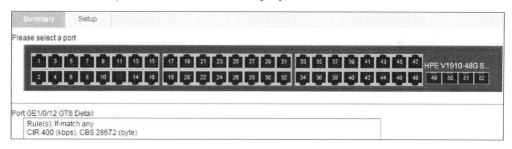

In order to test the bandwidth limitation setup, use the computer connected to a limited switch port, try to download a file and check the download speed.

After finishing the bandwidth limitation configuration, be sure to **save** your settings by clicking on the **Save** option available at the top right of the screen.

It is possible that some readers prefer to use the command-line instead of the web interface, therefore, we will also teach you how to configure traffic shaping using the command-line.

Using either the console, telnet or ssh, connect to the command-line of your switch and log in with a user who has administrative privileges.

If available to your switch model, enter ***the _cmdline-mode*** command in order to access the secret command-line mode of the device.

```
# _cmdline-mode on
```

Use the ***system-view*** command to enter the configuration mode.

```
# system-view
```

Access the desired network interface and configure the bandwidth limitation.

```
# interface GigabitEthernet1/0/12
# qos gts any cir 400
```

In our example, the network administrator restricted the switch port 12 to a maximum bandwidth of 50 Kilobytes.

Use the following command to check your configuration.

```
# display qos gts interface GigabitEthernet1/0/12
```

Save your settings by using the command below.

```
# save
```

To remove a bandwidth limitation, enter the configuration mode and use the following command.

```
# interface GigabitEthernet1/0/12
# undo qos gts any
```

Conclusion

This chapter taught using practical examples how to configure the traffic shaping feature, in order to help the network administrator achieve better control over the network bandwidth utilization.

Throughout this chapter, we were able to follow Luke while he configured a network switch to meet the following project requirements listed in the document called ***requirements of the new network***.

- It must be possible to limit the bandwidth used by a switch interface

At the end of this chapter, the reader should be able to configure the traffic shaper feature on a switch, in order to improve the control over his network.

To improve the learning curve, the following video were published on our youtube channel showing how to use the techniques presented in this chapter:

- HP Switch – Configure Traffic Shaper

– Chapter 14 –

DEVICE ISOLATION

Upon receiving a warning message from the antivirus management system reporting an infected computer on the network, Luke decided to investigate and discovered that the computer connected to port 13 is trying to infect others devices on the same network.

After analyzing the incident, Luke decided to use the device isolation technique to block the communication between end-user computers, in order to prevent the virus from spreading.

The use of techniques such as port isolation provides a quick way for a network administrator block the communication between two or more devices and therefore, increase his control over a network.

This chapter will teach how to perform the configuration of port isolation through a detailed step by step approach.

Throughout this chapter, the following tasks related to the implementation of the network project will be presented:

• How to isolate the communication between devices

All the lessons included in this chapter will be presented in a practical way using Luke's point of view during the implementation of his project.

Configuring Port Isolation

In our example, the network administrator will isolate the communication between the switch ports 13 and 14, in order to prevent the infected computer on port 13 to spread malwares to the computer connected to port 14.

Open the web interface, select the *Security* menu and click on the *Port Isolate Group* option to be sent to the port isolation configuration page.

To isolate the communication between switch ports, access the *Setup* tab, select the *Isolated port* option, select the desired ports and click on the *Apply* button.

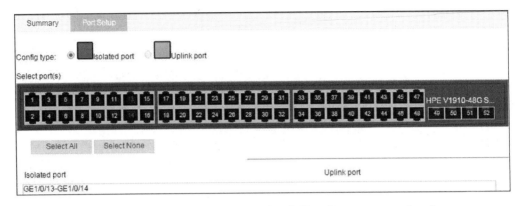

After finishing the port isolation setup, the following communication tests were performed by the network administrator, in order to validate the device isolation:

The communication between the computer connected to the switch port 13 and the computer connected to the port 14 was blocked by the port isolation configuration.

The communication between the computer connected to the switch port 13 and the computer connected to the port 15 were not blocked, because the port 15 was not a member of the port isolation configuration.

To check your settings, access the *Summary* tab and verify if the information displayed is correct.

After finishing the port isolation configuration, be sure to save your settings by clicking on the *Save* option available at the top right of the screen.

It is possible that some readers prefer to use the command-line instead of the web interface, therefore, we will also teach you how to configure port isolation using the command-line.

Using either the console, telnet or ssh, connect to the command-line of your switch and log in with a user who has administrative privileges.

If available to your switch model, enter the *_cmdline-mode* command in order to access the secret command-line mode of the device.

```
# _cmdline-mode on
```

Use the *system-view* command to enter the configuration mode.

```
# system-view
```

DEVICE ISOLATION

Apply the port isolation on the desired switch ports.

```
# interface GigabitEthernet1/0/13
# port-isolate enable

# interface GigabitEthernet1/0/14
# port-isolate enable
```

Use the following command to check your configuration.

```
# display port-isolate group
```

Save your settings by using the command below.

```
# save
```

To remove the port isolation, enter the configuration mode and use the following command.

```
# interface GigabitEthernet1/0/13
# undo port-isolate enable
```

Conclusion

This chapter taught using practical examples how to configure the port isolation feature, in order to help the network administrator achieve better control over the network traffic.

At the end of this chapter, the reader should be able to configure the isolation of devices connected to a switch, in order to improve the control over his network communication.

To improve the learning curve, the following video were published on our youtube channel showing how to use the techniques presented in this chapter:

- HP Switch – Port Isolation

– Chapter 15 –

VIRTUAL LABORATORY

After finalizing the implementation of the new network project successfully, Luke is aware that any change made improperly could completely paralyze the company's network environment and affect his credibility as a network administrator and project manager.

In order to reduce the likelihood of a network stoppage, Luke decides that before performing any new configuration on the network switches a test must be performed in a virtual environment as a validation phase.

This chapter will teach how to perform the creation of a virtual network laboratory through a detailed step by step approach.

Throughout this chapter, the following tasks related to the implementation of the network project will be presented:

• How to create a virtual network laboratory

All the lessons included in this chapter will be presented in a practical way using Luke's point of view during the implementation of his project.

Step by Step Guide

The virtual laboratory creation process is complex and requires full attention from the network administrator, in order to understand and perform the many steps required.

As the first step, the network administrator needs to perform the installation of the VirtualBox software which will provide the necessary basis to proceed with the installation of the network simulation software.

As the second step, the network administrator should perform the installation of the Wireshark software that will be able to offer features such as packet capture for eventual analysis.

As the third step, the network administrator should perform the installation of the HP Network Simulator software that will be responsible for providing the network simulation environment.

As the fourth and final step, we will show how to do a basic configuration of the network simulation software, such as adding devices, connecting devices and how to access virtual devices.

VIRTUAL LABORATORY

VirtualBox Installation

As the first step, the network administrator needs to install the VirtualBox software, therefore visit the *virtualbox.org* website and download *VirtualBox*.

After finishing the download, do a right-click on the VirtualBox installer and select the *Run as administrator* option in order to start the software installation.

The installation process itself is straightforward, therefore, just click on the *Next* button repeatedly until it is finished.

Welcome to the Oracle VM VirtualBox 5.0.14 Setup Wizard

The Setup Wizard will install Oracle VM VirtualBox 5.0.14 on your computer. Click Next to continue or Cancel to exit the Setup Wizard.

In our example, the VirtualBox software installation was performed on a computer running Windows 7, in order to create a virtual laboratory.

Wireshark Installation

As the second step, the network administrator needs to install the Wireshark software, therefore visit the *wireshark.org* website and download *Wireshark*.

After finishing the download, do a right-click on the Wireshark installer and select the *Run as administrator* option in order to start the software installation.

137

The installation process itself is straightforward, therefore, just click on the *Next* button repeatedly until the screen below is displayed, where the network administrator should select the *Install Winpcap option* and keep moving forward until the end of the installation.

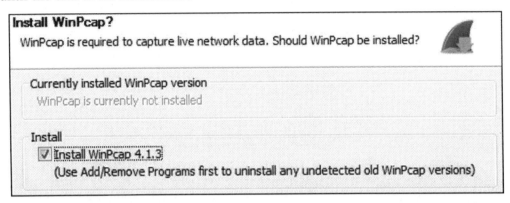

On the Install USBPcap screen, do not select the *Install USBPcap* option and click on the *Install* button.

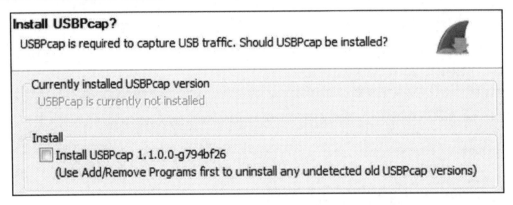

On the WinPcap installation screen, select the *Automatically start Winpcap driver at boot time* option and keep moving forward until the end of the installation.

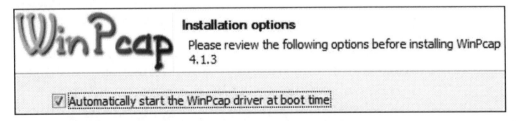

In our example, the Wireshark software installation was performed on a computer running Windows 7, in order to create a virtual laboratory.

VIRTUAL LABORATORY

HP Network Simulator Installation

As the third step, the network administrator needs to install the HP network simulator software, therefore visit the *hpe.com* website and download the *network simulator*.

After finishing the download, do a right-click on the file and select the *Extract all* option.

If the network administrator tries to install the HP network simulator software, he will see the following error message.

> The VirtualBox version is lower than the HCL needed. Please uninstalled the old version firstly, and reinstall HCL.

To solve the error above, open the windows registry editor as administrator and access the following registry key.

- HKEY_LOCAL_MACHINE > SOFTWARE > ORACLE > VIRTUALBOX

ab InstallDir	REG_SZ	C:\Program Files\Oracle\VirtualBox\
ab Version	REG_SZ	5.0.14
ab VersionExt	REG_SZ	5.0.14

As a workaround, change the value of the *VersionExt* option to 4.2.18 and exit the windows registry editor.

| ab Version | REG_SZ | 5.0.14 |
| ab VersionExt | REG_SZ | 4.2.18 |

After closing the registry editor, do a right-click on the HP Network Simulator installer and select the *Run as administrator* option in order to start the software installation.

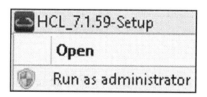

The installation process itself is straightforward, therefore, just click on the *Next* button repeatedly until it is finished.

139

After finishing the installation of HP Network Simulator software, open the windows registry editor as administrator, access the *VirtualBox* key, change the *VersionExt* option back to its original value and close the registry editor.

InstallDir	REG_SZ	C:\Program Files\Oracle\VirtualBox\
Version	REG_SZ	5.0.14
VersionExt	REG_SZ	5.0.14

In our example, the HP network simulator software installation was performed on a computer running Windows 7, in order to create a virtual laboratory.

Using the Network Simulator

To use the network simulator, open the start menu, do a right-click on the H3C Cloud Lab icon and select the *Run as administrator* option in order to start the software.

On the main screen, choose the device you want to insert and click on the screen, in order to add this device to the virtual laboratory.

In our example, the network administrator will add two virtual switches to demonstrate how to use the software, therefore, click on the *Switch icon* and then *click on the screen twice*.

VIRTUAL LABORATORY

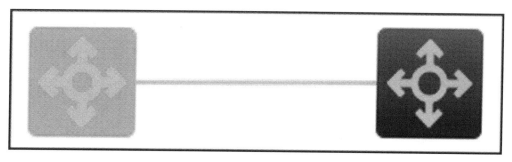

To do a communication test, two devices must be connected using a virtual link, therefore, right-click on a switch and select the *Add links* option.

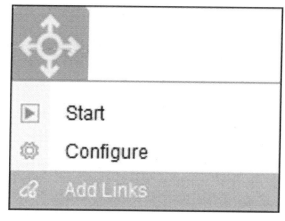

Click on the first virtual switch and then select the desired network interface.

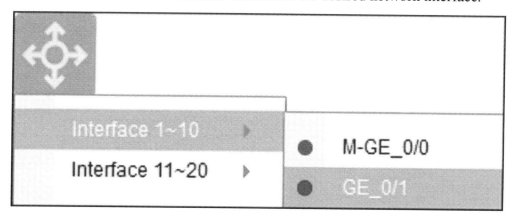

After selecting the desired network interface on the first virtual switch, click on the second virtual switch and select the desired network interface.

After finishing the connection between the virtual devices, click on the *Start all devices* button, in order to turn on all virtual devices that are members of this laboratory.

141

To access a virtual device console, right-click on a switch and select the *Start CLI* option.

A virtual switch comes without a configuration file, therefore, press the key sequence **[CTRL + D]**, in order to access the console of a new virtual switch.

```
Automatic configuration is running, press CTRL_D to break
# CTRL + D
Press ENTER to get started
```

After accessing the console of the first virtual switch, use the following commands to configure an IP address and save the configuration.

```
# system-view
# interface Vlan-interface 1
# ip address 192.168.0.1 255.255.255.0
# save
```

Access the console of the second virtual switch, use the following commands to configure an IP address and save the configuration.

```
# system-view
# interface Vlan-interface 1
# ip address 192.168.0.2 255.255.255.0
# save
```

To test connectivity between virtual devices, perform a ping from the first virtual switch to the IP address of the second virtual switch.

```
# ping 192.168.0.2
```

In our example, a basic configuration of the HP network simulator software was performed to demonstrate the connectivity between two virtual devices.

Conclusion

This chapter taught using practical examples how to configure a virtual laboratory in order to help the network administrator test his configurations before applying it to a production environment.

Throughout this chapter, we were able to follow Luke while he configured a virtual laboratory to meet the following project requirements listed in the document called ***requirements of the new network***.

• A virtual laboratory must be installed in order to test settings outside of the production environment

At the end of this chapter, the reader should be able to create a virtual laboratory, in order to prevent the use of untested configurations in the network production environment.

To improve the learning curve, the following video were published on our youtube channel showing how to use the techniques presented in this chapter:

• IIP Network Simulator – Installation on Windows

Afterword

Thank you for reading this book.

I would like to thank you, for sticking with me from the first chapter to the last.

Thank you so much to those who simply read, but a special thanks is reserved to those who helped me to promote the book through reviewing this material on Amazon. It means more than you know.

Writing this story helped me to become a better network administrator, and I hope it helps you too.

If you have any questions about the practices presented in this book, please feel free to reach out to me at:

- Youtube – www.youtube.com/c/fuckingit
- Website – www.fucking-it.com
- Facebook – www.facebook.com/fkingit/
- Twitter – twitter.com/_FuckingIT_

Please, share your thoughts about the book with someone who you think will benefit from reading it and take a moment to post a review online at Amazon.

Made in the USA
Lexington, KY
27 June 2018